Infant feeding
1990

A survey carried out by the Social
Survey Division of OPCS on behalf
of the Department of Health,
the Scottish Home and Health Department,
the Welsh Office and the Department
of Health and Social Services in Northern
Ireland

Amanda White
Stephanie Freeth
Maureen O'Brien

London: HMSO

© *Crown copyright 1992*
First published 1992
Second impression 1993 with amendments

ISBN 0 11 691443 2

The front cover shows the National Baby Care symbol

Acknowledgements

We would like to thank everybody who helped to make this survey possible. First of all, the other staff at Social Survey Division who contributed to the different stages of the survey. We would also like to thank staff in Vital Statistics Branch at OPCS, the GRO in Scotland and Northern Ireland who drew the sample for us, the staff in the Policy Planning and Research Unit of the Department of Finance and Personnel in Northern Ireland who conducted the field work in Northern Ireland, and the staff of the Department of Health and Social Services in Northern Ireland who processed part of the Northern Ireland data. We are grateful to the Working Party of the Panel on Child Nutrition for its valuable advice and criticism and support throughout the project. Finally we would like to thank the mothers who participated in the project, without whose cooperation the survey would not have been possible.

Contents

List of tables

viii

Chapter 3

Chapter 4

Chapter 5

Chapter 6

List of figures

Notes on the tables

Base numbers have been given in italics. Where a base number is less than 30, percentages have not been given but the actual number of cases is shown. Percentages of less than one per cent are shown as 0; cells with no cases are indicated by -. Due to rounding errors subtotals in some tables do not add up exactly to the total.

The varying positions of percentage signs and bases in the tables denote the presentation of different types of information. Where there is a percentage sign at the head of a column and the base at the foot the whole distribution is presented and the figures add up to 100%. Where there is no percentage sign in the table and a note in italics above the figures, the figures refer to the proportion of people who had the attribute being discussed and the complementary proportion (not shown in the table) who did not. In the more complex tables both the side and column headings define the group under discussion, the percentage indicating the proportion of the group who have a particular attribute .

Details of significance tests are not given in the report, but they have been carried out where appropriate. Differences referred to in the text are significant at the .05 level.

The term 'bottle fed' as used in this report refers to infants receiving infant formula. Some of the infants, particularly when they were older, would have been receiving infant formula from a lidded cup rather than a bottle.

Symbols used:
..   Not available
0   Denotes less than 0.5%
-     Denotes no cases

Summary of main findings and conclusions

Incidence and duration of breast feeding (Chapter 2)

Trends in the incidence of breastfeeding (section 2.1)

There has been no significant change in the incidence of breastfeeding in Great Britain since 1980. In 1990, 63% of mothers breastfed compared with 64% in 1985 and 65% in 1980. The lack of change in the incidence of breastfeeding was true for England and Wales, where the 1990 rate was 64%, compared with 65% in 1985 and 67% in 1980, and also for Scotland, where the incidence was 50% in 1990 compared with 48% in 1985 and 50% in 1980.

However, demographic characteristics of the mothers sampled in 1990 differ in some ways from those sampled in 1985, with more of them coming from subgroups with a higher rate of breastfeeding, older mothers and the better educated. Within certain subgroups, particularly women who left full-time education before the age of eighteen and mothers of first babies who were under the age of thirty when they gave birth, there has been a slight fall in the incidence of breastfeeding.

Factors associated with the incidence of breastfeeding (sections 2.1.1 -2.1.10)

The decline in the rate of breastfeeding among mothers of first babies between 1980 and 1985 has halted, with the 1990 incidence of 69% being the same as that for 1985.

As in all previous surveys a steep gradient in the incidence of breastfeeding can be seen, from 89% among mothers of first babies in Social Class I to 50% in Social Class V. Among women with no partner the incidence is even lower, at 47%.

The mother's level of education is also highly associated with her likelihood of breast feeding. Among women having their first child who left full-time education after the age of nineteen the incidence was 93%. This fell to 57% among women who left school aged 16 or under.

As in previous surveys, older women were more likely than younger women to breastfeed. Among women aged thirty or more having their first baby, the incidence of breastfeeding was 86%, compared with 39% among first mothers aged under 20.

The tendency for the incidence of breastfeeding to be higher in the South of the country, noted in previous surveys, is still apparent, with rates ranging from 74% in London and the South East to 50% in Scotland. In Northern Ireland the incidence was substantially lower than in the rest of the United Kingdom, at 36%. Previous experience of breastfeeding appears to have an important influence on how women feed subsequent babies. Among mothers of second and later babies, only 23% of those who had not breastfed their first child breastfed their latest baby, while among women who had breastfed a previous child for more than three months, 94% chose to breastfeed the latest child.

Although in 1990 there was an increased proportion of women in paid employment when the baby was less than ten weeks old, this has not had a detrimental effect on their willingness to breastfeed. As in 1985, mothers on maternity leave, whether paid or unpaid were more likely than all others to breastfeed, while those who were actually working at six weeks were as likely as those not working at all to have initially chosen to breastfeed.

Women who smoked before pregnancy were less likely than non-smokers to breastfeed, only 47% of them did so compared with 69% of non-smokers. This relationship held true for almost every social class group. Drinking, on the other hand, either before or during pregnancy, appears to have little effect on whether women breastfeed.

Prevalence of breastfeeding (section 2.2)

The overall prevalence of breastfeeding in Great Britain has shown virtually no change since 1985. The prevalence rates in England and Wales and in Scotland also show no change. By the time the babies were six weeks old only 50% of mothers were breastfeeding, and only a quarter (25%) of all mothers were breastfeeding at 4 months.

Trends in the duration of breastfeeding (section 2.3)

There has been no change between 1985 and 1990 in the length of time for which breastfeeding mothers continue to breastfeed, either in Great Britain as a whole or in England and Wales. In Scotland fewer women breastfed for as long as four months in 1990, 39% compared with 45% in 1985. Among women who started breastfeeding the most likely time for them to stop was in the first week after the birth, when 15% gave up. After this the proportion breastfeeding fell at a rate of between 2% and 6% each week for the first eight weeks.

Factors associated with the duration of breastfeeding (sections 2.3.1 - 2.3.9)

Mothers who continued to breastfeed longest were those who had previously breastfed a child, those in higher social classes, those who were educated beyond the age of eighteen, living in the south of the country, and non-smokers. There was no evidence to indicate that women who returned to work were breastfeeding for shorter periods than those who were not working. The picture is very similar to that in 1985.

Mothers in Northern Ireland who started breastfeeding continued to do so for a shorter time than those in the rest of the United Kingdom. By the time the babies were six weeks old, 62% of women in England and Wales who began breastfeeding were still doing so, compared with 60% in Scotland, but only 49% in Northern Ireland.

Influences on the choice of method of feeding (Chapter 3)

Choice of method of feeding (section 3.2)

Most women (93%) had decided on their method of feeding before the baby was born, and most of these (95%) carried out their intentions. Thirty-four per cent had planned to bottle feed and 59% to breastfeed, similar proportions to those of 1985. For women having a second or later child, their previous method of feeding exerted a strong influence on their method of feeding this baby, with few mothers who had bottle fed previous children choosing to breastfeed, and those who had previously breastfed for over six weeks being unlikely to choose bottle feeding this time around.

By far the most common reason given for planning to breastfeed, given by four fifths of those choosing this method, was that it is best for the baby. Over a third mentioned that breastfeeding was more convenient than bottle feeding. Among those choosing to bottle feed, almost two fifths did so because other people could feed the baby, while a similar proportion chose to bottle feed because they had done so before. Mothers of first babies choosing to bottle feed often said they did not like the idea of breastfeeding.

The way mothers' friends feed their babies also displays a strong relationship with the way they choose to feed their own babies, as does the way they were themselves fed as babies.

Contact with health professionals during the antenatal period (section 3.4)

Almost all mothers had received antenatal care during pregnancy. It is noteworthy that 12% had not been asked about how they intended to feed the baby, a figure that was the same for mothers of first and later babies. More mothers than in 1985 had discussed feeding at antenatal visits, 45% compared with 41%.

Fewer mothers (40%) had attended antenatal classes in 1990 than in 1985 (44%). This was true of both mothers having their first child and those having a second or subsequent baby.

Attendance was also strongly associated with social class, with women from the higher social classes being, in general, more likely to go to classes than those from the lower social classes. Attendance at antenatal classes was associated with a higher likelihood of intending to breastfeed, among women in both manual and non-manual social classes.

Influences on the duration of breastfeeding (Chapter 4)

Reasons for stopping breastfeeding (section 4.2)

The reasons given for stopping breastfeeding were broadly similar to those given in both 1980 and 1985. Insufficient milk was the most frequent reason given. During the first week, the most common reason for stopping was painful or engorged breasts. Only among mothers who breastfed for four months or more did 'breastfed for as long as intended' become the dominant reason for giving up.

Factors associated with giving up in the early weeks (sections 4.3 - 4.11

Since 1985 there has been a further decrease in the length of time mothers stayed in hospital after the birth, with over three quarters (74%) staying for five days or less, compared with just over half (51%) in 1985. Despite this, 12% of women who started breastfeeding had given up by the time they left hospital. Of the 20% of women who gave up in the first two weeks, only 8% did so after leaving hospital. These figures contradict the view that women breastfeed in hospital only to stop when they go home and find less help is available. The fact that the steepest drop in the duration of breastfeeding occurs during the first week after the birth suggests that the period in hospital is particularly important in establishing breastfeeding.

Events around the time of the birth and certain practices adopted in hospital were found to be associated with the probability of stopping breastfeeding in the early stages. Having a caesarian delivery under a general anaesthetic or having a low birthweight baby were both associated with early cessation of breastfeeding. Mothers whose babies received special care, however, were no more likely to stop breastfeeding in the first two weeks than other mothers. In 1990 the proportion of women who had caesarian sections with epidural anaesthesia had increased from the 1985 figure, and the proportion whose babies received special care was significantly lower than in 1985.

Delays in starting breastfeeding were associated with early cessation of breastfeeding. Only 12% of women who put the baby to the breast immediately gave up in the first two weeks, compared with 18% who delayed for up to an hour and rising to 34% of women who did not breastfeed until 12 hours or more after the birth.

In 1985, changes in hospital practices in relation to feeding schedules and the baby staying continuously at the mother's side were noted. These changes continued in 1990, with only 10% of mothers reporting having to feed at set times in hospital, compared with 19% in 1985, and 63% saying that the baby was with them continuously, compared to 47% in 1985. In addition, the practice of giving infant formula to breastfed babies, steady between 1980 and 1985 at 50% had fallen a little to 45% in 1990. Delays in initiating breastfeeding, feeding at set times, and offering infant formula to breastfed babies were all associated with early cessation of breastfeeding. Of all these practices, supplementing breastfeeding with bottles of infant formula shows the strongest association. Despite continuing changes in hospital practice, there was no resultant fall in the number of mothers who stopped breastfeeding in the first two weeks.

Present day practice in infant feeding: third report recommends that 'Those responsible for the care of the mother who intends to breastfeed and her baby encourage the practices associated with successful initiation of breastfeeding including early breastfeeding after birth, on-demand feeding, 'rooming-in' of mothers and babies, and the avoidance of complementary feeds or fluids of any sort'.

Problems with breastfeeding in the early weeks (sections 4.12 and 4.13)

The proportion of breastfeeding women reporting feeding problems in hospital increased between 1985 and 1990, from 30% in the earlier study to 36% in 1990. The most commonly reported problem was the baby not latching on to the breast, given by 31% of mothers who had problems, followed by sore or cracked nipples (30%). The vast majority of women with problems, 61%, said that help was always available in hospital when they needed it, and a further 33% said that it was generally available.

Of those still breastfeeding when they left hospital, 29% had stopped by six weeks after the birth. Of those who had experienced problems once they returned home 40% had stopped breastfeeding by six weeks, compared with 24% of those not experiencing problems. By far the most commonly reported problem at this stage, as in 1985, was that the baby was hungry. The incidence of this problem was lower, however, at 40% than it had been in 1985 when half of mothers reporting problems cited this.

Effects of friends and mothers (section 4.14)

There was a strong association between the duration of breastfeeding and the way the mother's friends fed their babies. Among women whose friends had mostly breastfed their babies, only 9% stopped breastfeeding during the first two weeks, compared with 28% of those whose friends mostly bottle fed. By six weeks after the birth only 20% of mothers with breastfeeding friends had stopped, compared with 51% of those whose friends bottle fed.

The way mothers were themselves fed as babies was also associated with the length of time they breastfed. At six weeks, 26% of breastfed mothers had stopped, compared with 46% of bottle fed mothers.

Infant formula and bottle feeding (Chapter 5)

The prevalence of bottle feeding

Although the majority of mothers started breastfeeding, 37% gave bottles from birth. By the time the babies were six weeks old 38% of those who began breastfeeding were now bottle feeding, while others were giving supplementary bottles of infant formula. Thus, by four weeks after the birth, the majority of babies in Great Britain were receiving infant formulas, and at four months three quarters of babies were fully bottle fed. The proportion of breastfed babies receiving additional bottles at six weeks has been rising since 1980, when it was 28%, to 34% in 1985 and 39% in the present survey. Thus although there has been little change in either the incidence or duration of breastfeeding since 1980, bottle feeding is becoming increasingly widespread as more mothers supplement breastfeeding with bottle feeds.

Advice about bottle feeding (sections 5.5 and 5.7)

Most mothers who attended antenatal classes had been shown how to make up a bottle (61%), a fall since 1985 when 69% had been taught. Mothers who intended to bottle feed were a little more likely than those planning to breastfeed to have been shown, 67% and 59% respectively.

As with breastfeeders, the most common problem experienced by bottle feeding mothers on their return home was that the baby appeared to be hungry. Of the 19% reporting problems, a third (33%) mentioned this one.

The use of non-human milk at different ages

In 1985 the most common type of infant formula given to babies at six weeks of age was whey dominant formula. In 1990 casein dominant formula had taken over at this stage, with 51% of mothers feeding this. The use of casein dominant formula rose to 61% at the four month stage, and fell to 33% at nine to ten months as mothers increasingly began to feed liquid cows milk. However, use of infant formula at this stage was more common in 1990 than it had been in 1985. Then, 32% were giving formula, compared with 57%. Conversely, in 1990, 42% were giving liquid cows milk at 9 to 10 months, compared with 67% in 1985.

At six weeks old and at four to five months old, breastfed babies who were receiving supplementary bottles were very much more likely to be given whey dominant formulas than were babies being exclusively bottle fed. The breastfed babies were also less likely to be receiving liquid cows milk at both the four to five month stage and at the 9 to 10 month stage than were the bottle fed babies.

Solid food, vitamins and other drinks (Chapter 6)

Trends in feeding practices (section 6.2)

Mothers in 1990, compared with those in 1985, were a little less likely to have introduced solid food to the baby before eight weeks of age (19% compared with 24% in 1985) but were a little more likely to have introduced them by the time the baby was three months old (68% compared with 62% in 1985). As in previous surveys, mothers who bottle fed tended to introduce solids at an earlier age than those who breastfed. *Present day practice in infant feeding: third report* states that very few infants will require solid food before the age of three months. Clearly, in 1990 the majority of mothers still began to feed solids earlier than is generally thought desirable.

Solid food given at different ages (section 6.3)

As in previous surveys, cereals and rusks were still the most common first solid foods. By about four months, when most of the babies were receiving solid food, commercial baby food was the most common food given. When asked what factors they took into account when deciding what solid food to give, the most frequent reply related to general nutrition. The presence of sugar, salt, vitamins and additives in the food were also commonly considered. Sugar was the most frequently avoided ingredient, generally because mothers view it as bad for the teeth.

Additional drinks (section 6.5)

Both breastfed and bottle fed babies were less likely to be given additional drinks in 1990 than they had been in 1985. Among breastfed babies the proportion being given additional drinks at six weeks was 58%, compared with 68% in 1985, and among bottle fed babies 89% were receiving additional drinks, compared with 94% in 1985. For all babies, 79% were receiving additional drinks in 1990 compared with 86% in 1985. The majority of mothers (59%) gave plain water at this stage, but a considerable minority (45%) were giving a herbal baby drink which contains sugar. Overall, however mothers in 1990 were less likely than in 1985 to give sweetened drinks, 50% did so, compared with 74% in 1985.

Supplementary vitamins (section 6.7)

There has been a considerable fall in the proportion of babies receiving supplementary vitamins at six weeks since 1980, when it was 47%, to 35% in 1985 and 12% in 1990. As young infants who are being breastfed or receiving infant formula are unlikely to become vitamin deficient this in itself is not a

matter for concern. However, *Present day practice in infant feeding: third report* recommends that 'vitamin supplementation should be given to infants and young children aged from six months up to at least two years and preferably five years'. By the time the babies were four months old, 19% were receiving supplementary vitamins, and at nine months, when most were being given a mixed diet and many were receiving cows milk rather than infant formula, only 30% were receiving supplementary vitamins, both substantial falls from 1985.

Problems with feeding (sections 6.8 and 6.9)

The proportion of mothers reporting problems with feeding declined as the baby got older, from 17% at four months old to 12% at nine months. At both stages, the most commonly reported problem was that the baby was ill, reported by 21% of mothers having problems at four months and 33% at nine months. Problems with feeding solids increased as the babies got older, with 11% reporting that the baby would not take solids at both stages, while 5% reported that the baby would take only certain solids at 4 months, rising to 21% at nine months. Reporting of this was lower, however, than in 1985, when 9% said the baby would only take certain solids at 4 months, and 29% at nine months.

In 1985, 32% of all mothers reported problems in finding somewhere to feed the baby when they went out, and the 1990 figure, at 30%, was only a little lower. However, compared with 1985, fewer mothers said they did not feed the baby in public places, 22% compared with 34% in 1985. Consequently more women reported no problems about feeding in public, 49% in 1990 compared with 34% in 1985.

Conclusion

The results of the survey indicate no increases in the incidence and duration of breastfeeding since 1985. Indeed, in some subgroups of the population, mothers of first babies in Social Class III (non-manual), mothers who left full-time education before the age of eighteen years, mothers under the age of thirty having their first babies, for example, there was a decrease in the incidence of breastfeeding. Added to this, a fifth of mothers who began breastfeeding stopped in the first few weeks of life. There has been no improvement in this proportion either. Changes in hospital practices, such as less delay in the initiation of breastfeeding, more demand feeding, less separation of mother and baby and fewer babies receiving supplementary bottles, have not so far been reflected in a smaller proportion of mothers giving up the attempt to breastfeed in the early weeks.

1 Introduction

1.1 Background to the survey

The 1990 Infant Feeding Survey is the fourth survey of infant feeding carried out by the Office of Population Censuses and Surveys on behalf of the Department of Health. The surveys were commissioned in response to the recommendation of the Committee on Medical Aspects of Food Policy (COMA) that provision should be made for 'a continuous review of patterns of infant feeding'. The first survey took place in 1975[1] and provided baseline statistics about infant feeding practices in England and Wales. The second and third surveys, in 1980[2] and 1985[3], also covered Scotland and have examined changes since 1975. The 1990 survey covered all four countries of the United Kingdom - England, Wales, Scotland and Northern Ireland. This report concentrates on infant feeding practices in Great Britain (England, Wales and Scotland) though some of the key results on Northern Ireland are presented in Chapter 7.[4]

In 1974, COMA set up a Working Party to review current practices in feeding normal infants and their effects on infants' well-being.[5] It concluded that all mothers should be encouraged to breastfeed their babies, preferably for four to six months, but at least for the first few weeks of life. It also concluded that the introduction of solid food before about four months should be discouraged.

Since this first report in 1974 there have been two further reports on infant feeding from COMA, in 1980[6] and 1988.[7] Both recommended that regular quinquennial surveys should continue and they endorsed the earlier recommendations.

1.2 Aims of the 1990 survey

Although there have been common aims since 1975 to all four surveys, each has some individual aims and the 1990 survey also covers some new topics not included in the previous surveys. Its main aims are:

a)   to establish how mothers feed their infants and what changes have occurred since 1985;

b)   to investigate changes in infant feeding in the early weeks and the factors associated with these changes; and

c)   to establish the age at which solid food is introduced and to examine weaning practices up to nine months.

1.3 Definitions used in the survey

A number of terms defined for the infant feeding surveys since 1975 are used throughout this report. The definitions are as follows:

Breastfed initially refers to all babies whose mothers put them to the breast at all, even if this was on one occasion only.

Incidence of breastfeeding is the proportion of sampled babies who were breastfed initially.

Still breastfed refers to all babies whose mothers were breastfeeding at all at a specified age, even if they were also bottle fed or receiving other food.

Prevalence of breastfeeding refers to the proportion of all sampled babies still being wholly or partially breastfed at specified ages.

Duration of breastfeeding is the length of time for which breastfeeding continued at all, regardless of when bottles or foods other than milk were introduced.

1.4 Design of the 1990 survey

An important factor governing the design of the 1990 survey was the need to be able to make comparisons with the previous surveys. Therefore the basic design was the same as for the 1985 survey. However, the 1985 and 1990 surveys differed from the 1975 and 1980 surveys in the following respects:

(i) *A larger sample of mothers was selected initially*

This was done partly because it was expected that changes in breastfeeding would be decreasing over time and so larger numbers would be required to detect significant changes in the subgroups of interest. This does not affect comparisons back to 1980 because the precision of the estimates of change is constrained by the smaller of the samples, but it will be important for future comparisons. Secondly, a larger sample allows more detailed examination of particular subgroups before the size of the group becomes too small for meaningful percentages to be calculated.

(ii) *Mothers in Social Class V as defined by the current or last occupation of the husband/partner or whose social class could not be classified were oversampled*

All the previous surveys had established strong associations between social class and various infant feeding practices: in general, mothers in the lower social class groups or with least formal education had the lowest rates of breastfeeding and those that started breastfeeding gave up soonest. They were also particularly likely to start giving their babies solid food earlier than other mothers. Since they form rather small groups in a random sample of mothers it was decided that the 1990 survey would replicate the procedure used in 1985 and gave mothers in Social Class V and those whose social class could not be classified twice the chance of selection compared with other mothers. In all the analyses presented in this report the results for these mothers have been downweighted by a factor of two to allow for this oversampling before they are added to results for other mothers. However, results can often be shown separately for these groups since their true numbers are greater than the reweighted base numbers.

(iii) *All mothers were followed up until nine months*

The 1975 and 1980 surveys had paid particular attention to feeding in the first half of infancy and while this information was still required, it was felt that the 1985 and 1990 surveys should collect more detailed information about later infancy. This led to the decision to ask more detailed questions about weaning foods and to follow up all mothers until their babies were at least nine months old, rather than just those who were breastfeeding at the previous contact, as had been done on the 1975 and 1980 surveys.

The main features of the sample design of the 1985 survey are described in the following section.

1.5 Sample design

The sample was designed to be representative of births occurring in England and Wales between 18 August and 14 September 1990 which had been registered within seven weeks of the birth. In Scotland the sample was of births occurring between 27 August and 13 October which had been registered within three weeks of the birth. The sample in Northern Ireland was of births occurring between 31 July and 8 October which had been registered within twelve weeks of the birth.

The sampling frame for England and Wales consisted of the draft birth registrations received by Vital Statistics Branch of OPCS. A sample of 100 registration sub-districts, grouped as necessary, was selected. As far as possible these were the same sub-districts as used on the 1975, 1980 and 1985 surveys. The sub-districts selected for the 1975 survey were selected with probability proportional to the number of births. But changes in the birth rates in a number of sub-districts necessitated some changes to the sub-districts selected since 1975. The criteria for the changes were determined by a procedure called the Keyfitz procedure.[8]

Within the selected sub-districts a systematic random sample of births was selected. Social class was coded on the basis of the information about the father's occupation recorded on the draft birth registration. The coding procedures normally used by Vital Statistics Branch were applied. All births coded as Social Class V or which were in the 'unclassified' category (mainly because the mother had no partner) were selected for

the survey. One in two of all other births were selected. Thus in total 6,467 births were selected for the survey in England and Wales.

In Scotland birth registrations are received by the General Register Office for Scotland and put onto computer within one week. This meant that computer rather than manual procedures could be used. Social class had already been coded and was shown on the computer print-out. It was therefore a simple matter to carry out the same procedure of rejecting every one in two births coded to Social Class I to IV as had been done in England and Wales. In Scotland a total of 2,597 births were selected.

The sampling frame for Northern Ireland consisted of the draft birth registrations received by the General Register Office for Northern Ireland. All births coded as Social Class V or which were in the 'unclassified' category (mainly because the mother had no partner) were selected for the survey. One in two of all other births were selected. In total, 2,041 births were selected for the survey in Northern Ireland.

Thus altogether a total of 9,064 births were selected in Great Britain (England, Wales and Scotland). In addition, with the 2,041 births selected in Northern Ireland, a total of 11,105 births were selected in the United Kingdom. As mentioned earlier this report concentrates on the results in England, Wales and Scotland and thus chapters one to six of the report present analysis based on the births in these three countries.

1.6 Procedure

1.6.1 England, Wales and Scotland

For the first stage 9,064 questionnaires were sent out during October and November 1990 to mothers of selected babies in England, Wales and Scotland. At this stage the babies were between six and ten weeks old. Those failing to reply after two weeks were sent a reminder letter and a second reminder was sent after a further two weeks if necessary. Interviewers were sent to contact mothers who had failed to reply after two reminder letters to encourage them to take part.

In January 1991 (when the babies were at least four months old) a second stage questionnaire was sent to all mothers who had completed the first questionnaire. As in stage 1, reminders were sent to those who had not responded and interviewers were sent to contact those who had failed to reply to the second reminder letter.

In June 1991 (when the babies were at least nine months old) a third stage questionnaire was sent to all those mothers who had completed the second stage questionnaire. Reminders were again sent as in stages 1 and 2, but interviewers were not sent out to contact the mothers who did not respond to the second reminder.

At both the second and third stages a small number of mothers were not contacted because although they had completed the previous stage they asked not to be contacted again. In addition, another small group of mothers were not approached because they had moved abroad.

1.6.2 Northern Ireland

Field work in Northern Ireland was carried out by the Policy Planning and Research Unit of the Department of Finance and Personnel of Northern Ireland. The field work procedure and timetable were similar to that used in Great Britain except that interviewers were sent out to contact mothers who did not respond to the second reminder at all three stages. The sample in Northern Ireland at stages one, two and three were respectively 2,041, 1,828 and 1,659.

1.7 Response

1.7.1 England, Wales and Scotland

At the first stage a sample of 9,064 babies was selected and the mothers approached by post. Those who failed to respond, even after two reminders, were contacted by interviewer. The overall response rate was 88%. Table 1.1 summarises the losses due to various sources of non-response.

Mothers were not asked to complete a questionnaire if they were separated from their baby for any reason (for instance if the baby had died, been adopted, or was in hospital). Such mothers were asked to indicate this on the front of the questionnaire and then to return the blank questionnaire so they would not be troubled again. Included in 'refusal' are those who returned a blank questionnaire with no explanation, as well as those explicitly refusing to co-operate. 'Post returned/not delivered' includes both questionnaires returned by the Post Office and those returned by someone other than the mother saying that she no longer lived at the address to which we had written. Wherever possible questionnaires were sent to any forwarding address given to us and every effort was made to provide a more detailed address where the Post Office required it in order to deliver the envelope.

At the second stage 7,894 mothers were written to again and a response rate of 90% was obtained. Details of the non-response are given in Table 1.2.

At the final stage 7,120 mothers were written to and 78% responded. Table 1.3 shows the details of the non-response.

Since at the second and third stages only mothers who had responded at the previous stage were contacted, the effect of non-response at each stage is cumulative. Table 1.4 shows the response at each stage as a proportion of the initial sample. Thus at the second stage questionnaires were received from 79% of the original sample, while by the third stage this proportion had fallen to 62%.

Table 1.1 Response rates and non-response at the first stage (six weeks or more) (1990)

	England and Wales		Scotland		Great Britain	
	No.	%	No.	%	No.	%
Initial response	6,467	100	2,597	100	9,064	100
Total response	5,732	89	2,218	85	7,950	88
due to postal enquiry	5,173	80	1,977	76	7,150	79
due to interviewer contact	559	9	241	9	800	9
Total non-response	735	11	379	15	1,114	12
baby not with mother	34	1	18	1	52	1
refusal	113	2	53	2	166	2
post returned/not delivered	114	2	56	2	170	2
no reply from postal stage and interviewer unable to contact	474	7	252	10	726	8

Table 1.2 Response rates and non-response at the second stage (four months or more) (1990)

	England and Wales		Scotland		Great Britain	
	No.	%	No.	%	No.	%
Second stage sample	5,732	100	2,218	100	7,950	100
Total response	5,159	90	1,980	89	7,139	90
due to postal enquiry	4,600	80	1,736	78	6,336	80
due to interviewer contact	559	10	244	11	803	10
Total non-response	573	10	238	11	811	10
refused at first stage	2	0	1	0	3	0
baby not with mother	4	0	3	0	7	0
refusal	92	2	32	1	124	2
post returned/not delivered	116	2	57	3	173	2
no reply from postal stage and interviewer unable to contact	310	5	141	6	451	6
did not approach because mother and baby had moved abroad	49	1	4	0	53	0

3

Table 1.3 Response rates and non-response at the third stage (nine months or more) (1990)

	England and Wales		Scotland		Great Britain	
	No.	%	No.	%	No.	%
Third stage sample	5,159	100	1,980	100	7,139	100
Total response	4,056	79	1,521	77	5,577	78
Total non-response	1,103	21	459	23	1,562	22
refused at second stage	10	0	3	0	13	0
baby not with mother	4	0	2	0	6	0
refusal	18	0	13	0	31	0
post returned/not delivered	106	2	39	2	145	2
no reply	958	19	402	20	1,360	19
did not approach because mother and baby had moved abroad	7	0	0	0	7	0

Table 1.4 Summary of response at the three stages (1990)

	England and Wales		Scotland		Great Britain	
	No.	%	No.	%	No.	%
Initial sample	6,467	100	2,597	100	9,064	100
Response at stage 1	5,732	89	2,218	85	7,950	88
Response at stage 2	5,159	80	1,980	76	7,139	79
Response at stage 3	4,056	63	1,521	59	5,577	62

Table 1.5 Response rates and non-response in Northern Ireland (1990)

	Stage 1 (six weeks or more)		Stage 2 (four months or more)		Stage 3 (nine months or more)	
	No.	%	No.	%	No.	%
Initial sample	2,041	100	1,828	100	1,659	100
Total response	1,828	90	1,659	91	1,506	91
due to postal enquiry	1,535	75	1,253	69	1,182	71
due to interviewer contact	293	14	406	22	324	20
Total non-response	213	10	169	9	153	9
refused at last stage	0	-	1	0	3	0
baby not with mother	5	0	5	0	2	0
refusal	125	6	75	4	57	3
post returned/not delivered	10	0	11	1	22	1
no reply from postal stage and interviewer unable to contact	73	4	77	4	69	4

1.7.2 Northern Ireland

In Northern Ireland 2,041 mothers were selected and contacted at the first stage and 90% responded. At the second stage the 1,827 mothers who cooperated at stage 1 were contacted again and 91% responded. Finally the 1,656 mothers who participated at stage 2 were written to at stage 3 and 91% cooperated. Table 1.5 sets out the details of the non-response in Northern Ireland for all three stages. As was the case in Great Britain the effect of non-response at each stage in Northern Ireland is cumulative. Thus at the second stage questionnaires were received from 81% of the original sample, while by the third stage this proportion had fallen to 74%.

1.8 Reweighting the results

In order to obtain a sufficiently large sample of births in Scotland and Northern Ireland for separate analysis, births in the two countries were given a greater chance of selection than those in England and Wales. So that results for Scotland could be added in their correct proportion to those for England and Wales when producing figures for Great Britain, the Scottish results were reweighted by a factor of 0.238. Similarly, to enable the results for Northern Ireland to be added in the correct proportion to those of Great Britain to give figures for the United Kingdom in Chapter 7, the Northern Ireland results were reweighted by a factor of 0.08.

As babies born to mothers in Social Class V or whose social class was unclassifiable had been given twice the chance of selection compared with other babies, the results for these mothers had to be reweighted by a factor of 0.5 to make them comparable with the results of other mothers.

Applying regional and social class reweighting factors to the main stage sample gives a total weighted sample of 5,413 questionnaires for Great Britain, made up of 4,942 questionnaires for England and Wales and 471 questionnaires for Scotland. The weighted sample for the United Kingdom is 5,533 which is made up of 4,942 questionnaires for England and Wales, 471 questionnaires for Scotland and 120 questionnaires for Northern Ireland. When the results for Scotland and Northern Ireland are shown separately in this report these are based on a larger weighted sample of 1,981 Scottish mothers and 1,497 mothers in Northern Ireland. These enhanced samples which are large enough to give reliable national estimates for Scotland and Northern Ireland, have been weighted only to take into account the over-sampling of the lower social class groups.

Data obtained from the second and third stage questionnaires required additional reweighting to adjust for the non-response to each of these stages. The reweighting factors were calculated to take account of the differing levels of response obtained from mothers in different social class groups and to arrive at the same weighted sample as at the first stage questionnaire (5,413). This was done to facilitate comparisons between different tables and parts of tables. However, calculations of sampling errors and tests of significance have been based on the actual number of questionnaires rather than on the weighted totals shown in the tables. All tables displaying data from the second and third stages include percentages based on a smaller number of individuals than is suggested by the weighted base presented. These tables have been marked to draw attention to the fact that such percentages are subject to larger errors than those based on data at the first stage.

1.9 Making comparisons with the 1985 results

One of the main purposes of the 1990 survey was to provide data to establish trends in infant feeding. There are several factors affecting comparisons made over time and before we present the results it is important to consider their effect on the interpretation of the data. First, sample size is a major determinant of the capacity to measure change. Because of this, the sample was designed to be sufficiently large for comparisons to be made for the important subgroups.

Second, it must be remembered that each survey was based on an independent random sample of individuals. Thus the two sets of results are each subject to sampling error and this becomes particularly important when the data are presented for small subgroups. When sampling errors are taken into account an apparent change with time may be seen to be not statistically significant.

Third, both surveys are subject to possible biases due to non-response. Sampling from draft birth registrations meant, however, that a certain amount of information was available about the babies whose mothers did not take part in the survey and this information can be used to validate the sample. In addition, comparisons of the composition of the 1990 sample with 1990 population estimates indicate that the 1990 sample of mothers had a similar age structure to the women who gave birth to a baby in 1990, and the birth order distribution of the 1990 sample was similar to that for legitimate live births in Great Britain. The social class composition of the 1990 sample and the 1990 population of women who gave birth to a baby were also comparable. Details of the sample validation carried out are presented in Appendix I.

Fourth, any significant differences between the composition of the 1985 sample and the 1990 sample will affect the comparison over time. Details of the composition of each of the samples are given in Appendix I. On the whole the two samples had very similar characteristics in terms of birth order, mother's main occupation and geographical distribution. However, the 1990 sample of mothers differed from the 1985 sample in three respects. First, the mothers in the 1990 sample were older than mothers in the 1985 sample. The last two columns of Table 1.6 show that 31% of the 1990 mothers were aged 30 years or over compared with 27% in 1985; 25% of the mothers were aged between 20 and 24 years in 1990 compared with 30% in 1985. Second, compared to 1985, a

Table 1.6 Distribution of the sample by mother's age, for first and later births (1980, 1985 and 1990 Great Britain)

Mother's age	First births			Later births			All babies*		
	1980	1985	1990	1980	1985	1990	1980	1985	1990
	%	%	%	%	%	%	%	%	%
Under 20	15	16	13	2	2	2	8	8	7
20-24	40	38	31	24	23	20	31	30	25
25-29	33	31	36	38	38	39	36	35	37
30 or over	12	14	20	36	38	39	25	27	31
	100	100	100	100	100	100	100	100	100
Base:	1,831	2,347	2,430	2,377	2,875	2,983	4,224	5,223	5,413

* Includes some cases for whom the exact birth order was not known.

Table 1.7 Distribution of the sample by age at which mother completed full-time education, for first and later births (1980, 1985 and 1990 Great Britain)

Age at which mother completed full-time education	First births			Later births			All babies*		
	1980	1985	1990	1980	1985	1990	1980	1985	1990
	%	%	%	%	%	%	%	%	%
16 or under	59	56	49	66	63	57	63	60	54
17 or 18	25	30	35	19	23	30	21	26	32
Over 18	16	14	16	15	14	13	16	14	14
	100	100	100	100	100	100	100	100	100
Base:	*1,831*	*2,347*	*2,430*	*2,377*	*2,875*	*2,983*	*4,224*	*5,223*	*5,413*

* *Includes some cases for whom the exact birth order was not known.*

Table 1.8 Distribution of the sample by social class as defined by current or last occupation of husband/partner for first and later births (1980, 1985 and 1990 Great Britain)

Social class	First births			Later births			All babies*		
	1980	1985	1990	1980	1985	1990	1980	1985	1990
	%	%	%	%	%	%	%	%	%
I & II	25	25	26	28	26	27	26	26	26
IIINM	10	9	8	7	8	8	8	8	8
All non-manual	35	34	34	35	34	35	34	34	34
IIIM	40	30	28	43	33	31	42	32	30
IV & V	15	16	14	16	21	17	16	19	16
All manual	55	46	42	59	54	48	58	51	46
Unclassified	10	3 ⎤ 20	5 ⎤ 23	6	4 ⎤ 12	6 ⎤ 17	8	4 ⎤ 15	6 ⎤ 20
No husband/partner		16 ⎦	18 ⎦		7 ⎦	11 ⎦		11 ⎦	14 ⎦
	100	100	100	100	100	100	100	100	100
Base:	*1,831*	*2,347*	*2,430*	*2,377*	*2,875*	*2,983*	*4,224*	*5,223*	*5,413*

* *Includes some cases for whom the exact birth order was not known.*

Table 1.9 Distribution of the population and the sample by mother's age (1980, 1985 and 1990 Great Britain)

Mother's age	Population*			Surveys		
	1980	1985	1990	1980	1985	1990
	%	%	%	%	%	%
Under 20	9	9	8	8	8	7
20-24	31	30	26	31	30	25
25-29	34	35	36	36	35	37
30 or more	26	27	31	25	27	31
	100	100	100	100	100	100
Base:	*725,000*	*723,100*	*772,073*	*4,224*	*5,223*	*5,413*

* *Figures based on all live births.*

smaller proportion of the 1990 mothers left school at the age of 16 years; 54% compared with 60% and a larger proportion left school between the age of 17 and 18 years; 32% compared with 26% (last two columns of Table 1.7). Third, there has been an overall increase in the proportions of mothers with no partner and those whose social class could not be classified. Table 1.8 shows the distribution of the total sample by social class overall, and separately for mothers of first births and of later births. The eighth and ninth columns of Table 1.8 indicate that the proportion of mothers not living with a husband or partner rose from 11% in 1985 to 14% in 1990, and the proportion of mothers whose social class could not be classi-

fied increased slightly from 4% in 1985 to 6% in 1990. This increase occurred both among mothers of first births and among mothers of later births.

The observed differences between the 1985 and 1990 samples reflect national changes in the demographic composition of women who had a baby between 1985 and 1990. Table 1.9 shows the age of mothers in the 1985 and 1990 samples and the age of women who had a baby in Great Britain in the same two years. The table shows that the age profile of the mothers in the 1990 sample matches the age profile of women who had a baby in 1990. In addition, a comparison of the national age profile of women who had a baby in 1985 and 1990 reveals that the pattern and extent of the changes noted between the 1990 and 1985 samples were replicated nationally. The fourth row of Table 1.9 shows that the proportion of women who gave birth to a baby at age 30 years and over in Great Britain rose from 27% in 1985 to 31% in 1990, exactly the same as the difference found in the 1985 and 1990 Infant Feeding Surveys. The second row of Table 1.9 indicates that the proportion of women who gave birth to a baby at ages of between 20 to 24 years fell from 30% in 1985 to 26% in 1990; the decline revealed when the 1985 and 1990 Infant Feeding Surveys were compared was from 30% to 25%. The increase in the proportion of mothers not living with a husband or partner revealed when the 1985 and 1990 samples were compared has also been evident in the results of other OPCS surveys. The General Household Survey found that in 1980 lone mothers made up 10% of the population of Great Britain, by 1985 it had reached 12% and the figure for 1990 was 17%. These increases in the proportion of mothers not living with a husband or partner found by the General Household Survey were comparable with those found in the 1985 and 1990 Infant Feeding Surveys.

In summary, this section has shown that the 1990 Infant Feeding Survey sample is representative of women who had given birth to a baby in 1990. A comparison of the 1990 and 1985 samples shows differences in the age and education level of the mothers, and slight variations in the proportion of mothers not living with a husband or partner or whose social class could not be classified. All the differences detected reflect national changes in the demographic composition of women who had given birth to a baby between 1985 and 1990. Nevertheless, when making comparisons between 1985 and 1990 one should bear in mind the differences found between the 1985 and 1990 samples, namely, the decline in the proportion of mothers who left full-time education aged under 19 years, increased proportion of mothers in the older age groups, those whose social class could not be classified, and those not living with a husband/partner.

References

[1] Jean Martin. *Infant feeding 1975: attitudes and practices in England and Wales*. HMSO (1978).

[2] Jean Martin and Janet Monk. *Infant feeding 1980*. HMSO (1982).

[3] Jean Martin and Amanda White. *Infant feeding 1985*. HMSO (1988).

[4] For detailed information on the survey in Northern Ireland contact Dr E McWhirter of the Department of Health and Social Services, Social Statistics and Research Branch, Castle Buildings, Stormont, Belfast, BT4 3UD.

[5] *Present day practice in infant feeding*. Report on Health and Social Subjects 9. DHSS (1974).

[6] *Present day practice in infant feeding 1980*. Report on Health and Social Subjects 20. DHSS (1980).

[7] *Present day practice in infant feeding: third report*. Report on Health and Social Subjects 32. DHSS (1988).

[8] Nathan Keyfitz. Sampling with probabilities proportional to size: adjustment for changes in the probabilities. *J. Amer. Assn.* 46 (1951), pp 105-109.

2 Incidence and duration of breastfeeding

2.1 Incidence of breastfeeding

As on the previous surveys incidence of breastfeeding is defined as 'the proportion of babies who were breastfed initially'. This includes all babies who were put to the breast at all, even if this was on one occasion only. Although it can be argued that putting a baby to the breast on only one or two occasions does not really constitute breastfeeding, this definition has the advantage of being clear cut and avoids the decision about a necessarily arbitrary criterion of a certain number of attempts or a certain length of time as constituting breastfeeding. Moreover, this survey, like the previous three, found that very few mothers stop breastfeeding after only a few attempts and so the results would be little changed if a more stringent definition were used.

Table 2.1 sets out the incidence of breastfeeding since 1975. It shows that there had been a dramatic increase in the incidence of breastfeeding between 1975 and 1980, from 51% to 67%, but since 1980 the incidence rate has levelled off; 65% in 1985 and 64% in 1990. Similarly in Scotland the rates have remained steady at 50% in 1980, 48% in 1985 and 50% in 1990. Thus there appears to have been little change in the incidence of breastfeeding between 1980 and 1990 in either England and Wales or Scotland (Figure 2.1).

Table 2.1 also shows that in 1990 the incidence of breastfeeding in Great Britain was 63%. This compares with a figure of 64% in 1985 and does not represent a statistically significant change between the two surveys. However Chapter 1 points out that the sample of mothers in 1990 differed slightly in characteristics from the sample of mothers in 1985. Compared with the 1985 sample the 1990 sample had a higher proportion of mothers aged 30 years and over, a lower proportion of mothers who completed full-time education aged 16 years and under and a higher proportion of mothers not living with a husband or partner or whose social class could not be classified. These differences in the composition of the 1985 and 1990 samples reflected the changes in the demographic composition of the population of women who had a baby between 1985 and 1990. All the previous surveys and later sections of

this chapter show that older mothers and mothers who completed full-time education over the age of 16 years are more likely to breastfeed. As the 1990 sample had a higher proportion of these mothers it is possible that the incidence of breastfeeding had remained unchanged since 1985 because mothers in 1990 were more likely to have come from subgroups in the population who tend to breastfeed. To assess this a standardised figure was calculated to indicate what the incidence of breastfeeding in 1990 would have been if the 1990 sample of mothers had the same age structure and educational background as the 1985 sample. (Although there were social class differences between the 1985 and 1990 samples social class was not included in the standardisation because preliminary investigations showed that the differences in social class between the two samples did not significantly affect the incidence of breastfeeding.) The standardised incidence of breastfeeding in 1990 for Great Britain was 60%, slightly lower than the 1985 figure of 64%. This indicates that although there was no actual difference in the incidence of

Figure 2.1 Incidence of breastfeeding by country (1975, 1980, 1985 and 1990)

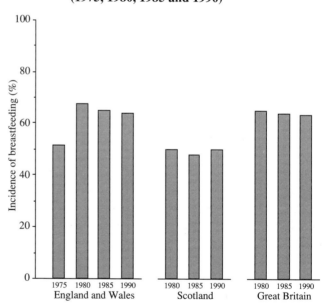

Table 2.1   Incidence of breastfeeding by country (1975, 1980, 1985 and 1990)

	England and Wales				Scotland*			Great Britain		
	1975	1980	1985	1990	1980	1985	1990	1980	1985	1990
Percentage who breast fed initially	51	67	65	64	50	48	50	65	64	63
Base:	*1,544*	*3,755*	*4,671*	*4,942*	*1,718*	*1,895*	*1,981*	*4,224*	*5,223*	*5,413*

* *The data for Scotland are weighted to give a national estimate.*

Table 2.2 Incidence of breastfeeding by birth order (1980, 1985 and 1990 Great Britain)

Birth order	1980	1985	1990	1980	1985	1990
	Percentage who breastfed initially			*Bases:*		
First birth	74	69	69	*1,831*	*2,347*	*2,430*
Second birth	60	60	59	*1,519*	*1,725*	*1,690*
Third birth	56	57	58	*558*	*737*	*835*
Fourth or later birth	49	56	52	*281*	*387*	*413*
All second and subsequent births*	58	59	58	*2,377*	*2,875*	*2,983*

* Includes some cases for whom exact birth order was not known.

Figure 2.2 Incidence of breastfeeding by birth order (1980, 1985 and 1990 Great Britain)

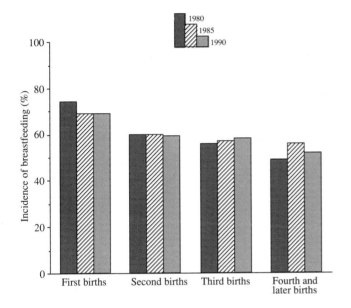

breastfeeding between 1985 and 1990 this was because the 1990 population of women having a baby was more likely to have come from subgroups who tend to breastfeed. As the next few sections show, within certain subgroups separately there was in fact evidence of a downward trend.

In all the previous surveys birth order and social class as defined by the current or last occupation of the mother's husband/partner were shown to be strongly associated with rates of breastfeeding. We next examine whether these relationships persist in 1990 and whether the incidence of breastfeeding in the different subgroups has changed since 1985.

2.1.1 Incidence of breastfeeding and birth order

The previous surveys showed the highest incidence of breastfeeding was found among mothers of first babies, with successively lower rates for higher birth orders. Table 2.2 and Figure 2.2 indicate that this was again the case in 1990.

The previous surveys demonstrated that the likelihood of a mother breastfeeding a second or subsequent baby depended crucially on her experience of feeding her first baby. Few mothers who have chosen not to breastfeed their first child will

reverse the decision with subsequent children. The 1985 survey showed that there had been a decline in breastfeeding since 1980 among mothers having their first baby, and raised the concern that the fall might herald a decrease in breastfeeding among these mothers in subsequent years. However, Table 2.2 shows that there has not been a decrease in breastfeeding among mothers having their second or subsequent baby between 1985 and 1990. The rate has remained virtually the same between 1985 and 1990 at 59% and 58% respectively. The rate for first babies has also remained stable between 1985 and 1990; 69% in both years.

2.1.2 Incidence of breastfeeding and social class (as defined by the current or last occupation of the mother's husband/partner)

The analyses in Chapter 1 used information from the birth registration details about the husband or partner's occupation to assign social class. In analysing the survey results in this and later chapters the information given on the questionnaires has been used as it usually gave more detail. In the questionnaire mothers were asked whether they were married or living with a partner and questions were asked about the partners's occupation to enable social class to be coded.

The social class gradient in breastfeeding, with the highest rates among mothers in the highest social classes, was clearly established in all the previous surveys and Figure 2.3 indicates that it was still apparent in 1990. Taking 1990 figures for all births it can be seen that there was a particularly large difference between Social Class III Non-manual (73%) and Social Class III Manual (59%) (Table 2.3). The lowest rates of breastfeeding were among mothers not living with a husband or partner (43%) and Social Class V (41%). The incidence of breastfeeding among mothers in different social class groups was very similar in 1990 to that observed in 1985. The only noticeable difference between 1990 and 1985 was a decline in breastfeeding among mothers of first babies in the Social Class III (non-manual) group: 85% had breastfed in 1985 compared with only 76% in 1990.

2.1.3 Incidence of breastfeeding and age at which mother completed full-time education

In 1990, as in previous years, mothers who left full-time education at the statutory school-leaving age (16 years for

Figure 2.3 Incidence of breastfeeding by social class as defined by current or last occupation of husband/partner (1980, 1985 and 1990 Great Britain)

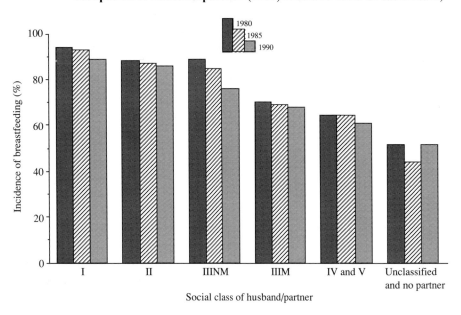

Table 2.3   Incidence of breastfeeding by social class as defined by current or last occupation of husband/partner for first and later births (1980, 1985 and 1990 Great Britain)

Social class of husband/partner	First birth			Later births			All babies		
	1980	1985	1990	1980	1985	1990	1980	1985	1990
	Percentage who breastfed initially								
I	94	93	89	83	83	84	87	87	86
II	88	87	86	71	76	74	78	81	79
IIINM	89	85	76	65	68	70	77	76	73
All non-manual	90	88	85	73	75	74	80	81	79
IIIM	70	69	68	52	55	53	59	61	59
IV	64	68 · 64	63 · 61	43	51 · 48	47 · 45	52	58 · 54	53 · 52
V		50	50		38	36		43	41
All manual	68	67	66	50	52	50	57	58	57
Unclassified	51	59 · 44	66 · 51	54	53 · 43	57 · 45	52	55 · 44	61 · 48
No partner		41	47		37	38		39	43
All babies	74	69	69	58	59	58	65	64	63

Bases:									
I	138	136	191	196	171	207	335	307	398
II	311	444	447	457	584	605	769	1,028	1,052
IIINM	179	213	200	175	223	227	355	436	427
All non-manual	628	793	838	828	978	1,039	1,459	1,771	1,877
IIIM	742	703	684	1,022	962	927	1,769	1,666	1,611
IV	266	284	306	391	453	430	659	738	736
V		103	39		144	78		247	117
All manual	1,009	1,090	1,029	1,413	1,559	1,435	2,428	2,651	2,464
Unclassified	195	81	126	136	125	187	336	207	313
No partner		383	437		212	322		595	760
All babies	1,831	2,347	2,430	2,377	2,875	2,983	4,224	5,223	5,413

10

Table 2.4 Incidence of breastfeeding by age at which mother completed full-time education and whether first or later births (1980, 1985 and 1990 Great Britain)

Age at which mother completed full-time education	First birth			Later births			All babies		
	1980	1985	1990	1980	1985	1990	1980	1985	1990
	Percentage who breastfed initially								
16 or under	65	58	57	48	49	46	55	53	50
17 or 18	81	80	75	70	70	68	76	75	71
Over 18	94	94	93	85	86	88	89	89	91
All babies*	74	69	69	58	59	58	65	64	63
Bases:									
16 or under	*1,067*	*1,310*	*1,184*	*1,562*	*1,800*	*1,697*	*2,632*	*3,110*	*2,881*
17 or 18	*453*	*698*	*839*	*438*	*648*	*871*	*892*	*1,346*	*1,710*
Over 18	*298*	*328*	*387*	*358*	*397*	*388*	*657*	*725*	*775*
All babies*	*1,831*	*2,347*	*2,430*	*2,377*	*2,875*	*2,983*	*4,224*	*5,223*	*5,413*

* Includes some cases where mother's age at finishing full-time education was not known.

Figure 2.4 Incidence of breastfeeding by mother's education (1980, 1985 and 1990 Great Britain)

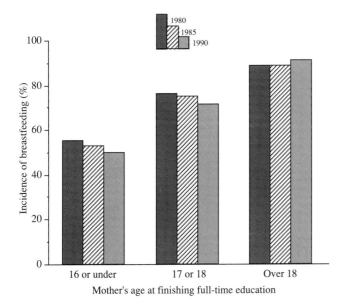

most of these women) were least likely to breastfeed, while those who had continued in education beyond 18 years were most likely to do so.

Table 2.4 and Figure 2.4 compare the rate of breastfeeding between 1980, 1985 and 1990 and show a fall in the rate of breastfeeding among mothers who left full-time education at or before the age of 18 years. The rate for mothers who left full-time education at 16 years or under dropped from 53% in 1985 to 50% in 1990 and the rate for those who left full-time education between the age of 17 and 18 years fell from 75% in 1985 to 71% in 1990. The decrease was most marked among mothers of first babies who left full-time education at this age for whom the rate fell from 80% in 1985 to 75% in 1990.

2.1.4 Incidence of breastfeeding and mother's age

A mother's age at the birth of second and subsequent children depends on her age at the first birth, the number of children she has had and the spacing between them. It is therefore difficult to interpret the significance of any relationship between

breastfeeding and the age of mothers of second and later babies. For this reason analysis of the effect of mother's age is confined to mothers of first babies.

In 1990, as in previous years, mothers who had their first birth aged 30 years or over were the most likely to breastfeed while mothers who had their first baby under the age of 20 years were the least likely to do so (Table 2.5 and Figure 2.5).

Table 2.5 Incidence of breastfeeding by mother's age (first births only, 1980, 1985 and 1990 Great Britain)

Mother's age	1980	1985	1990	*1980*	*1985*	*1990*
	Percentage who breastfed initially			*Bases:*		
Under 20	47	42	39	*280*	*380*	*315*
20-24	69	65	61	*739*	*898*	*756*
25-29	87	81	77	*598*	*729*	*874*
30 or over	86	86	86	*211*	*337*	*479*
All first babies*	74	69	69	*1,831*	*2,347*	*2,430*

* Includes some cases where mother's age was not known.

Figure 2.5 Incidence of breastfeeding first babies by mother's age (1980, 1985 and 1990 Great Britain)

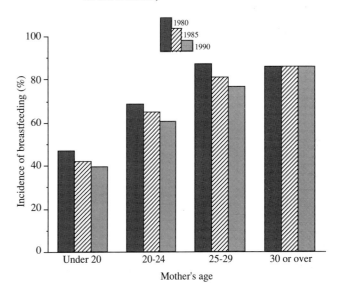

Table 2.6 Incidence of breastfeeding by sex of baby and country (1990)

Sex of baby	England and Wales	Scotland*	Great Britain
	Percentage breastfed initially		
Boys	64	49	63
Girls	63	52	62
All babies	64	50	63
Bases:			
Boys	*2,518*	*1,001*	*2,756*
Girls	*2,419*	*976*	*2,651*
All babies†	*4,937*	*1,981*	*5,413*

* *The data for Scotland are weighted to give a national estimate.*
† *Includes some cases for whom sex was not known.*

Figure 2.6 Incidence of breastfeeding by region (1980, 1985 and 1990 Great Britain)

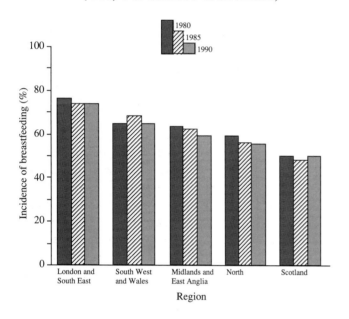

It was pointed out earlier that the incidence of breastfeeding among mothers of first babies had remained unchanged at 69% since 1985. However, Table 2.5 and Figure 2.5 reveal a slight decrease in the rate of breastfeeding among mothers who were under the age of 30 years when they had their first baby. However, this decrease did not reduce the overall rate of breastfeeding for mothers of first babies. This was probably because the proportion of mothers aged 30 years and over having their first baby (the group with the highest rate of breastfeeding) had grown since 1985 (see Chapter 1 for details). This increase means that these mothers had a larger effect on the overall rate of breastfeeding in 1990 than in 1985 and the increased effect counterbalanced the decline in breastfeeding among younger mothers.

2.1.5 *Incidence of breastfeeding and sex of baby*

The sex of the baby was recorded in 1990 to assess whether feeding practices differ according to the sex of the baby. Table 2.6 shows that for Great Britain as a whole as well as in England and Wales and Scotland the sex of the baby had no effect on whether the mother started breastfeeding. Mothers who had baby boys were just as likely to start breastfeeding as mothers who had baby girls. The effect of the baby's sex on the prevalence and duration of breastfeeding will be examined in later sections.

2.1.6 *Incidence of breastfeeding and region*

The previous surveys demonstrated a decline in breastfeeding rates as one moves northwards through the country. Table 2.7 and Figure 2.6 show that this picture was still apparent in 1990, ranging from 74% in London and the South East to 50% in Scotland.

Table 2.7 Incidence of breastfeeding by region (1980, 1985 and 1990 Great Britain)

Region	First birth			Later births			All babies		
	1980	1985	1990	1980	1985	1990	1980	1985	1990
	Percentage who breastfed initially								
London and South East	85	81	78	69	69	70	76	74	74
South West and Wales	75	74	75	59	63	58	65	68	65
Midlands and East Anglia	73	66	67	56	59	53	63	62	59
North	68	63	61	52	50	50	59	56	55
Scotland	57	53	56	46	45	45	50	48	50
All babies*	74	69	69	58	59	58	65	64	63
Bases:									
London and South East	*574*	*747*	*795*	*708*	*928*	*990*	*1,284*	*1,675*	*1,785*
South West and Wales	*197*	*298*	*275*	*286*	*359*	*391*	*483*	*657*	*666*
Midlands and East Anglia	*345*	*419*	*447*	*458*	*541*	*594*	*808*	*960*	*1,041*
North	*518*	*628*	*689*	*654*	*750*	*763*	*1,179*	*1,378*	*1,452*
Scotland	*722*	*875*	*949*	*989*	*1,020*	*1,032*	*1,718*	*1,895*	*1,981*
*All babies**	*1,831*	*2,347*	*2,430*	*2,377*	*2,875*	*2,983*	*4,224*	*5,223*	*5,413*

* *The data for Scotland are weighted to give a national estimate.*

Table 2.8 Incidence of breastfeeding among mothers of more than one child according to length of time for which first child was breastfed (1980, 1985 and 1990 Great Britain)

Length of time for which first child was breastfed	1980	1985	1990	1980	1985	1990
	Percentage who breastfed initially			Bases:		
First child bottle fed	28	25	23	953	1,066	1,099
1 week or less	45	45	43	197	338	230
More than 1 week, up to two weeks	55	59	59	160	123	149
More than 2 weeks, up to 4 weeks	68	65	68	151	167	149
More than 4 weeks, up to 6 weeks	76	75	78	154	194	179
More than 6 weeks, up to 3 months	90	85	84	230	326	339
More than 3 months, up to 6 months	91	95	94	245	271	287
More than 6 months	96	94	97	292	415	449
All second and subsequent babies*	58	59	58	2,377	2,875	2,983

* Includes some cases where details of feeding first child were not known.

Table 2.7 compares the 1990 figures with those for 1985 and shows that there has been a drop in the incidence of breastfeeding among mothers of later births in the Midlands and East Anglia, and in the South West and Wales since 1985 (from 59% to 53% in the Midlands and East Anglia and from 63% to 58% in the South West and Wales). This resulted in a slight fall in the overall rate for these two regions since 1985. The situation in the other regions has remained unchanged since 1985.

2.1.7 Incidence of breastfeeding and previous experience of breastfeeding

As mentioned earlier, whether or not a mother breastfeeds a second or subsequent baby is significantly affected by her experience of feeding her first child. This is shown clearly in Table 2.8. Only 23% of mothers who had not breastfed their first child breastfed their latest baby, compared with 94% of those who had breastfed an earlier child for more than three months.

The situation in 1990 is very similar to that in 1985, the only notable difference being that mothers who breastfed their first child for more than six months were even more likely to breastfeed their current baby in 1990 than in 1985: 97% in 1990 compared with 94% in 1985 (Table 2.8).

In addition Table 2.8 reveals that the picture in 1990 was also very similar to that of 1980, this indicates that the effect of previous experience does not appear to have changed since 1980. This is in contrast to the changes noted between 1975 and 1980 when it was found that mothers who had not previously breastfed, or had only done so for a short time, were less deterred from trying again in 1980 than their counterparts in 1975. Although it cannot be expected that many women who choose to bottle feed their first child will subsequently change to breastfeeding, it still seems that women who have tried breastfeeding are being deterred from trying again if the first experience is not very successful.

2.1.8 Incidence of breastfeeding and mother's employment status at about six weeks

At the time of completing the Stage 1 questionnaire when their babies were about six to ten weeks old, mothers were asked whether they were doing any paid work or whether they were on paid or unpaid maternity leave. Table 2.9 shows that in 1990 8% of the mothers were in paid work when their baby was between six and ten weeks old. About one fifth were on paid maternity leave and another 5% were on unpaid maternity leave. Table 2.9 also shows that there has been an increase in the proportion of women in paid work when their baby was less than ten weeks old. The increase among women on paid maternity leave was even bigger. It has been suggested that the increased proportions of women working when their children are very young might affect the proportion of mothers who choose to breastfeed. As in 1985 the 1990 survey results show no evidence to support this. Table 2.10 (see overleaf) shows that the situation in 1990 was very similar to that in 1985, namely that mothers on maternity leave were more likely than other mothers to breastfeed (this was the case both among mothers of first babies and of later babies), and similar proportions of mothers in paid work and who were not working at around six weeks had breastfed initially; 59% and 58% respectively. Thus both the 1990 and 1985 results indicate that an early return to work does not significantly deter women from breastfeeding initially (the effect of returning to work on the duration of breastfeeding will be examined later).

Table 2.9 Mother's working status when the babies were between six and ten weeks old (1980, 1985 and 1990 Great Britain)

Mother's working status	1980	1985	1990
	%	%	%
Working	4	5	8
On maternity leave – paid	⎤ 8	6	21
unpaid	⎦	6	5
Not working	88	83	66
All mothers	100	100	100
Bases:	4,224	5,223	5,413

13

Table 2.10 Incidence of breastfeeding by mother's working status (1980, 1985 and 1990 Great Britain)

Mother's working status		First births*		Later births*		All babies		
		1985	1990	1985	1990	1980	1985	1990
		Percentage who breast fed initially						
Working		72	66	57	54	64	63	59
On maternity leave –	paid	80	77	75	72	⎱ 82	79	76
	unpaid	85	77	65	77	⎰	80	77
Not working		66	63	58	55	63	61	58
All babies†		69	69	59	58	65	64	63
Bases:								
Working		*103*	*164*	*173*	*268*	*173*	*276*	*432*
On maternity leave – paid		*219*	*816*	*76*	*324*	⎱ *337*	*295*	*1,140*
unpaid		*260*	*185*	*78*	*89*	⎰	*338*	*274*
Not working		*1,760*	*1,259*	*2,529*	*2,295*	*3,699*	*4,289*	*3,554*
All babies†		*2,347*	*2,430*	*2,875*	*2,983*	*4,224*	*5,223*	*5,413*

* *1980 figures not available.*
† *Includes some cases where mother's working status was not known.*

Table 2.11 Proportion of mothers who smoked before pregnancy, during pregnancy, and who gave up during pregnancy, by social class as defined by current or last occupation of husband/partner (1985 and 1990 Great Britain)

Social class	Percentage of mothers who smoked:				Base: all mothers		Percentage of mothers who gave up smoking during pregnancy		Base: those who smoked before pregnancy	
	before pregnancy		during pregnancy							
	1985	1990	1985	1990	*1985*	*1990*	1985	1990	*1985*	*1990*
I	16	17	8	8	*307*	*398*	51	50	*49*	*66*
II	26	23	18	13	*1,028*	*1,052*	32	41	*268*	*237*
IIINM	28	26	19	16	*436*	*427*	35	41	*124*	*113*
IIIM	41	40	31	29	*1,666*	*1,611*	25	37	*683*	*636*
IV	41	45	32	34	*738*	*736*	23	24	*303*	*333*
V	53	47	46	39	*247*	*117*	13	17	*130*	*54*
No partner	64	62	53	53	*595*	*760*	17	16	*381*	*474*
Unclassified	45	39	38	29	*207*	*313*	15	26	*93*	*122*
Total	39	38	30	28	*5,223*	*5,413*	24	27	*2,031*	*2,035*

2.1.9 Incidence of breastfeeding and smoking

The 1990 as well as the 1985 survey found that high social class was correlated with low smoking rate before pregnancy and high rates of giving up the habit during pregnancy. Table 2.11 shows that in 1990 the proportion of mothers who smoked before pregnancy was virtually the same as in 1985, 38% compared with 39%. However in 1990 rather more mothers gave up smoking during pregnancy than had done previously (27% compared with 24%) and hence rather fewer smoked during pregnancy (28% compared with 30%). The decline in smoking during pregnancy since 1985 occurred in all social class groups except mothers in Social Class I who had the lowest smoking rate, and mothers who tended to have the highest smoking rate; those in Social Class IV and those not living with a husband or partner.

Just over 80% of the mothers who were smokers before pregnancy were given advice or information on the effect of smoking during pregnancy. It is therefore interesting to assess if the decrease in smoking was related to the advice and information smokers received. Table 2.12 suggests that advice

Table 2.12 Changes to smoking habits in pregnancy among smokers and whether they had advice on smoking during pregnancy (1990 Great Britain)

Changes to smoking habits during pregnancy	Smokers who had advice on smoking in pregnancy	Smokers who had no advice on smoking in pregnancy	All mothers who smoked before pregnancy*
	%	%	%
Stopped smoking during pregnancy	24	43	27
Continued smoking during pregnancy	76	57	73
Base:	*1,638*	*388*	*2,035*

* *Includes some cases where it is not known if the mother received advice on smoking.*

on smoking did not seem to make a woman give up smoking during pregnancy. In 1990, only 24% of the smokers who received advice on smoking gave up the habit while a higher proportion (43%) of smokers who had not received any advice stopped smoking. This negative relationship between advice on smoking and stopping smoking is apparent in every social class group.

Table 2.13 Sources of information on smoking during pregnancy (1990 Great Britain)

Percentage of smokers who:	
	%
received information on smoking	81
received no information on smoking	19
Base: all smokers	*2,035*

Source of information on smoking	Percentage who received information from each source*
Printed material	48
Midwife or nurse	68
Friend or relative	37
Doctor	67
Health visitor	18
Others	3
Base: smokers who received information on smoking during pregnancy	*1,638*

* *Percentages add up to more than 100 as some mothers received information from more than one source.*

Table 2.14 The effect of various sources of information on smoking in changing smoking habits during pregnancy (1990 Great Britain)

Source of information on smoking	Percentage who received information from source and stopped smoking	Base:
Printed material	28	777
Midwife or nurse	21	1,121
Friend or relative	20	611
Doctor	20	1,097
Health visitor	18	297
Others	24	45

Table 2.13 reveals that smokers received information on the effect of smoking during pregnancy from a range of sources. Over two thirds of them were given such information from midwives or nurses, or doctors, just under half obtained the information from printed material, and over a third received information from friends or relatives.

Although printed material was not the most common source of information on smoking in pregnancy it seems to be the most effective means of persuading smokers to stop smoking during pregnancy. Table 2.14 shows that 28% of the smokers who received information from printed material gave up, while between 18% to 24% of women who had information from the other common sources stopped smoking.

The 1990 survey found that, overall and in every social class group, smoking during or before pregnancy was associated with a lower incidence of breastfeeding. Table 2.15 shows that over two thirds (69%) of women who did not smoke during pregnancy began breastfeeding, while only 46% of those who smoked during pregnancy started breastfeeding. The incidence of breastfeeding was higher for non-smokers in every social class group; the only exception being women in Social Class III non-manual who smoked before pregnancy (the rate in this group was similar to that for those who did not smoke before pregnancy). Tables 2.11 and 2.15 taken together show that the higher rate of giving up smoking during pregnancy was not followed by changes in the incidence of breastfeeding among non-smokers or smokers during pregnancy; the rate of breastfeeding among both groups has hardly changed since 1985, if anything it has gone down slightly among non-smokers during pregnancy.

Table 2.15 Incidence of breastfeeding by smoking and social class as defined by current or last occupation of husband/partner (1985 and 1990 Great Britain)

Social class	Proportion of women who started breastfeeding initially							
	Smoking status before pregnancy:				Smoking status during pregnancy:			
	Non-smoker		Smoker		Non-smoker		Smoker	
	1985	1990	1985	1990	1985	1990	1985	1990
I	88	88	81	80	89	87	70	78
II	85	82	69	70	84	81	66	67
IIINM	82	73	62	74	80	74	59	66
IIIM	66	64	53	52	65	64	50	48
IV	62	63	51	42	64	60	45	41
V	49	45	39	36	50	48	35	30
No partner	45	49	36	39	48	50	32	37
Unclassified	64	68	44	50	67	68	35	42
Total	71	70	52	51	71	69	46	46
Bases:								
I	*258*	*291*	*49*	*53*	*282*	*317*	*24*	*26*
II	*760*	*667*	*268*	*166*	*846*	*739*	*182*	*94*
IIINM	*312*	*228*	*124*	*83*	*355*	*267*	*81*	*44*
IIIM	*983*	*623*	*683*	*328*	*1,153*	*730*	*513*	*221*
IV	*435*	*252*	*303*	*141*	*504*	*290*	*234*	*103*
V	*117*	*28*	*130*	*19*	*134*	*34*	*113*	*14*
No partner	*214*	*140*	*381*	*186*	*280*	*179*	*315*	*147*
Unclassified	*114*	*129*	*93*	*61*	*127*	*152*	*79*	*38*
Total	*3,193*	*2,358*	*2,031*	*1,037*	*3,682*	*2,708*	*1,541*	*687*

Table 2.16 Proportion of mothers who drank alcohol before pregnancy, during pregnancy and who gave up during pregnancy by social class as defined by current or last occupation of husband/partner (1990 Great Britain)

Social class	Percentage of mothers who drank alcohol:		Base: all mothers	Percentage of mothers who gave up drinking alcohol during pregnancy	Base: those who drank alcohol before pregnancy
	before pregnancy	during pregnancy			
I	90	70	398	22	357
II	89	72	1,052	20	940
IIINM	87	69	427	20	371
IIIM	87	68	1,611	22	1,403
IV	83	63	736	24	613
V	81	63	117	22	95
No partner	85	67	760	21	644
Unclassified	73	58	313	21	229
Total	86	67	5,413	22	4,652

Table 2.17 Estimated weekly alcohol consumption of mothers who drank during pregnancy by social class as defined by current or last occupation of husband/partner (1990 Great Britain)

Units of alcohol consumed per week	Social class								All drinkers
	I	II	IIINM	IIIM	IV	V	No partner	Unclassified	
	%	%	%	%	%	%	%	%	%
Less than 1 unit	73	76	76	71	71	68	64	78	72
1-7 units	25	22	23	25	25	28	27	17	24
8-14 units	2	2	1	3	3	3	6	4	3
15 units or more	0	1	0	1	2	2	2	1	1
Base:	278	752	295	1,095	463	74	506	179	3,642

2.1.10 Incidence of breastfeeding and drinking alcohol

Mothers were asked for the first time in 1990 whether they drank any alcohol before, during and after pregnancy. The bottom row in Table 2.16 reveals that 86% drank some alcohol before pregnancy of whom 22% gave up alcohol completely while they were pregnant; thus 67% of all the women in the sample drank some alcohol during pregnancy. However most of the women who continued drinking alcohol during pregnancy drank lightly. This is discussed later in Table 2.17.

Table 2.16 shows that there were clear social class differences in drinking behaviour before and during pregnancy in 1990. Women from the higher social class groups were more likely to drink alcohol before pregnancy than women in the lower social class groups (90% of women in Social Class I drank alcohol before pregnancy compared with 81% in Social Class V). Women whose social class could not be classified were least likely to drink alcohol and women not living with a husband or partner were more likely to drink than women in Social Class IV and V. The rate of giving up alcohol during pregnancy was very similar in all the social class groups though women in Social Class IV were marginally more likely to stop drinking during pregnancy; 24% compared with between 20% and 22% in the other groups (Table 2.16). Thus the social class differences in drinking behaviour before pregnancy were maintained during pregnancy.

Looking at the 'All drinkers' column in Table 2.17 indicates that 72% of those who drank during pregnancy (48% of the 5,413 women in the sample) drank less than one unit a week,

24% of those who drank alcohol during pregnancy (16% of the whole sample of mothers) drank between 1 and 7 units, 3% of drinkers (2% of the whole sample) drank between 8-14 units, and 1% drank 15 units or more (ie more than the recommended safe level for women who are not pregnant). Women not living with a husband or partner were the heaviest drinkers during pregnancy; 6% of these women drank between eight to fourteen units a week compared with between 1% and 4% in the other social class groups. (Table 2.17).

As with giving up smoking, the decision to stop drinking alcohol during pregnancy did not seem to be related to whether a woman had had advice or information on the effect of alcohol during pregnancy. Table 2.18 indicates that in 1990, 22% of all drinkers stopped drinking during pregnancy. Drinkers who

Table 2.18 Changes to drinking habits in pregnancy among drinkers and whether they had advice on drinking alcohol during pregnancy (1990 Great Britain)

Changes to drinking habits during pregnancy	drinkers who received advice on drinking in pregnancy	drinkers who did not receive advice on drinking in pregnancy	All mothers who drank before pregnancy*
	%	%	%
Stopped drinking during pregnancy	21	23	22
Continued drinking during pregnancy	79	77	78
Base:	2,995	1,624	4,652

Includes some cases where it is not known if the mother received advice on drinking in pregnancy.

16

Table 2.19 Sources of information on drinking alcohol during pregnancy (1990 Great Britain)

Percentage of drinkers who:

	%
received information on drinking alcohol	65
received no information on drinking alcohol	35
Base: all drinkers	*4,652*

Source of information on drinking alcohol	Percentage who received information from each source*
Printed material	52
Midwife or nurse	60
Friend or relative	22
Doctor	49
Health visitor	14
Others	2
Base: drinkers who received information on drinking alcohol during pregnancy	*2,993*

* *Percentages add up to more than 100 as some mothers received information from more than one source.*

Table 2.20 The effect of various sources of information on drinking alcohol in changing drinking habits during pregnancy (1990 Great Britain)

Source of information on drinking alcohol	Percentage who received information from source and stopped drinking	Base:
Printed material	20	*1,556*
Midwife or nurse	21	*1,803*
Friend or relative	22	*644*
Doctor	21	*1,454*
Health visitor	21	*426*

did not receive advice on the effect of alcohol during pregnancy were just as likely to stop drinking (23%) as those who had received advice on the impact of alcohol (21%). This pattern was evident in all the social class groups.

In 1990 women received information on the effect of alcohol in pregnancy from a range of sources. Table 2.19 shows that the majority of drinkers received information from midwives (60%). Printed material and doctors were also common sources (respectively 52% and 49% of drinkers had advice from these two sources), while 22% of drinkers obtained advice from friends and relatives and 14% received advice from health visitors.

Table 2.20 indicates that around 20% of those who received information on the effect of alcohol during pregnancy gave up the habit when they were pregnant. None of the sources stood out as particularly more effective than the others in persuading drinkers to stop drinking alcohol during pregnancy. This was the case in all the social class groups.

Table 2.21 sets out the breastfeeding rates of the mothers according to their drinking pattern before and during pregnancy. Looking at all the mothers together the 'Total' row of the first three columns in the table shows that in 1990 women who drank more than one unit a week during pregnancy (labelled as 'drinkers') were just as likely to breastfeed as those who did not drink during pregnancy. However, women who drank less than one unit a week during pregnancy (labelled as 'light drinkers') were more likely to breastfeed; 66% of light drinkers breastfed compared with 61% of non-drink-

Table 2.21 Incidence of breastfeeding by drinking and social class as defined by current or last occupation of husband/partner (1990 Great Britain)

Social class	Proportion of women who started breastfeeding initially				
	Drinking status during pregnancy:			Drinking status before pregnancy:	
	Non-drinker	Light drinker*	Drinker†	Non-drinker	Drinker
I	87	88	83	93	86
II	77	81	79	85	79
IIINM	76	70	75	79	72
IIIM	57	63	54	53	60
IV	50	59	48	51	54
V	34	44	44	33	42
No partner	44	45	39	51	42
Unclassified	61	60	60	64	59
Total	61	66	58	62	63
Bases:					
I	*120*	*199*	*79*	*40*	*357*
II	*300*	*557*	*195*	*112*	*940*
IIINM	*132*	*215*	*80*	*56*	*371*
IIIM	*516*	*747*	*348*	*208*	*1,403*
IV	*273*	*312*	*151*	*123*	*613*
V	*43*	*47*	*27*	*22*	*95*
No partner	*253*	*301*	*205*	*116*	*644*
Unclassified	*134*	*131*	*48*	*84*	*229*
Total	*1,770*	*2,510*	*1,133*	*761*	*4,652*

* *Light drinkers are women who drank less then one unit a week during pregnancy.*
† *Drinkers are women who drank one unit of alcohol or more a week during pregnancy.*

ers and 58% of drinkers. However, this pattern was not evident in every social class group. The pattern of breastfeeding and drinking habits among women in Social Classes III manual and IV was similar to the pattern described above, but in the other social class groups light drinkers were just as likely to breastfeed as drinkers and non-drinkers.

The last two columns in Table 2.21 show that women who drank alcohol before pregnancy were just as likely to breastfeed as women who did not drink alcohol before they were pregnant (63% of drinkers breastfed compared with 62% of non-drinkers). Among women in Social Classes III manual, IV and V there was a tendency for drinkers to be more likely than non-drinkers to breastfeed. Among the other social class groups the opposite was true, non-drinkers were more likely than drinkers to breastfeed (Table 2.21). However, none of these differences were statistically significant. Thus Table 2.21 suggests that in 1990 overall, and in Social Classes III manual and IV, women who drank less than one unit a week during pregnancy were more likely to breastfeed; in the other social class groups drinking habits during pregnancy had no effect on breastfeeding rates. Drinking habits before pregnancy also did not seem to affect breastfeeding rates.

2.1.11 Estimating the incidence of breastfeeding

The results in the earlier sections of this chapter have shown

that the incidence of breastfeeding is associated with socio-demographic variables such as birth order, social class, mother's education level, region, etc. These socio-demographic variables are interrelated, thus account must be taken of the interrelationships before the relationship of these factors with the incidence of breastfeeding can be determined.

One method of examining the relationship between two variables while controlling for their relationships with other variables is the use of crosstabulations, for example, examining the incidence of breastfeeding by social class within each region. However, this method is of limited use with small samples as the numbers in many of the cells are too small for meaningful percentages to be calculated. The three previous infant feeding surveys solved this problem by examining standardised rates of breastfeeding based on estimates of breastfeeding rates produced by a statistical procedure called the maximum likelihood procedure. Standardised rate of breastfeeding for a particular socio-demographic variable is a rate standardised for the effects of the other interrelated variables. The maximum likelihood procedure involves fitting a model to the data from which the most probable relationship between each variable and incidence of breastfeeding can be determined. The procedure produces estimates of the incidence of breastfeeding for each of the subgroups included. These estimates are what one would expect to find if average values are obtained from a large

Table 2.22   Estimated incidence of breastfeeding for total sample (1990 Great Britain)

Birth order	Mothers age at finishing full-time education	Region	Social class as defined by current or last occupation of husband/partner					
			I	II	IIINM	IIIM	IV & V	Unclassified
			Percentage who breast fed initially					
First births	16 or under	London & SE	85	81	76	68	63	57
		SW & Wales	80	74	69	60	55	48
		Midlands	78	72	67	58	52	45
		North	74	68	62	52	47	40
		Scotland	66	60	53	43	38	32
	17 or 18	London & SE	92	89	87	81	78	73
		SW & Wales	89	86	82	75	71	65
		Midlands	88	84	80	74	69	63
		North	85	81	77	69	65	58
		Scotland	80	75	70	61	56	49
	Over 18	London & SE	97	96	95	93	91	88
		SW & Wales	96	95	93	90	88	85
		Midlands	96	94	93	89	87	84
		North	95	93	91	87	84	80
		Scotland	92	90	87	82	79	74
Later births	16 or under	London & SE	77	71	66	56	51	44
		SW & Wales	70	63	57	47	42	36
		Midlands	68	62	35	45	40	33
		North	63	56	50	40	35	29
		Scotland	54	47	41	31	27	22
	17 or 18	London & SE	87	83	80	72	68	62
		SW & Wales	83	76	73	65	60	53
		Midlands	81	72	71	62	57	50
		North	78	72	69	57	52	45
		Scotland	71	64	58	46	43	36
	Over 18	London & SE	95	94	92	89	86	83
		SW & Wales	93	91	89	85	82	77
		Midlands	93	91	88	83	80	75
		North	91	89	86	80	76	71
		Scotland	88	84	81	73	69	63

number of random samples of births throughout Great Britain. The maximum likelihood procedure takes account of the interrelationships between all the variables and eliminates chance fluctuations due to small numbers in some cells.

In 1990 the maximum likelihood procedure was carried out on the Great Britain sample (Northern Ireland was excluded). In order to make comparisons with 1985, the analysis in 1990 used the same variables, namely, birth order, social class, age at which the mother completed her full-time education and region.

The estimates of the incidence of breastfeeding for each of the subgroups included in the maximum likelihood procedure are shown in Table 2.22. The estimates show that the highest rate of breastfeeding (97%) would be expected among mothers who were educated beyond the age of eighteen years, whose husband had professional or managerial occupations (Social Class I), whose babies were their firstborn child and whose babies were born in London and the South East. Mothers from this group were also estimated to have the highest rate of breastfeeding in 1975, 1980 and 1985. At the other extreme, the lowest rate of breastfeeding (22%) would be expected among mothers who left school aged sixteen years or under, who had no partner or whose partner's occupation could not be classified, whose babies were the second or subsequent child and whose babies were born in Scotland. This group was also estimated to have the lowest rate of breastfeeding in 1985.

From the results of the maximum likelihood procedure it is possible to obtain standardised rates of breastfeeding for each variable in turn, standardising for the effects of the other interrelated variables. For example, the standardised rates of breastfeeding for first births and for second and subsequent births are those which would be expected if the two categories were identical in composition in terms of mother's education level, social class and region. Tables 2.23 to 2.26 show the standardised incidence of breastfeeding for each of the four main variables. The standardised incidence figures for first and later births are largely similar to the unstandardised rates, but for the other variables standardisation has reduced the range of results found in the different subgroups. Despite this reduction, the standardised rates are still significantly different for each subgroup. This was also the case in 1985 and 1980. This indicates that although some of the apparent differences between subgroups were due to interrelationships between the variables, all four variables (birth order, social class, mother's education level and region) were independently related to the incidence of breastfeeding in 1990, as well as in 1985 and 1980.

2.2 Prevalence of breastfeeding

Prevalence of breastfeeding refers to the proportion of babies still breastfed at specific ages, even if the babies were also receiving infant formula or solid food. Even though there has been little change in the incidence of breastfeeding between

Table 2.23 Estimated incidence of breastfeeding by birth order, standardised for social class as defined by current or last occupation of husband/partner, mother's education and region, compared with the unstandardised rate (1990 Great Britain)

Birth order	Standardised	Unstandardised
	Percentage who breastfed initially	
First births	68	69
Later births	58	58

Table 2.24 Estimated incidence of breastfeeding by social class as defined by current or last occupation of husband/partner, standardised for birth order, mother's education and region, compared with the unstandardised rate (1990 Great Britain)

Social class	Standardised	Unstandardised
	Percentage who breastfed initially	
I	79	86
II	75	79
IIINM	70	73
IIIM	62	59
IV and V	57	52
Unclassified and no partner	51	48

Table 2.25 Estimated incidence of breastfeeding by mother's education, standardised for birth order, social class as defined by current or last occupation of husband/partner, and region, compared with the unstandardised rate (1990 Great Britain)

Mother's age at finishing full-time education	Standardised	Unstandardised
	Percentage who breastfed initially	
16 or under	54	50
17 or 18	69	71
Over 18	86	91

Table 2.26 Estimated incidence of breastfeeding by region, standardised for birth order, social class as defined by current or last occupation of husband/partner and mother's education, compared with the unstandardised rate (1990 Great Britain)

Region	Standardised	Unstandardised
	Percentage who breastfed initially	
London and South East	71	74
South West and Wales	64	65
Midlands and East Anglia	62	59
North	58	55
Scotland	50	50

Table 2.27   Prevalence of breastfeeding at ages up to nine months by country (1980, 1985 and 1990)

Region	England and Wales			Scotland*			Great Britain		
	1980	1985	1990	1980	1985	1990	1980	1985	1990
	Percentage breastfeeding at each age								
Birth	67	65	64	50	48	50	65	64	63
1 week	58	56	54	44	41	41	57	55	53
2 weeks	54	53	51	41	38	39	52	51	50
6 weeks	42	40	39	32	29	30	41	38	39
4 months	27	26	25	21	22	20	26	26	25
6 months	23	21	21	18	18	16	22	21	21
9 months	12	11	12	9	9	9	12	11	11
Base:	*3,755*	*4,671*	*4,942*	*1,718*	*1,895*	*1,981*	*4,224*	*5,223*	*5,413*

* *The data for Scotland are weighted to give a national estimate.*

Figure 2.7   Prevalence of breastfeeding at ages up to nine months (1980, 1985 and 1990 Great Britain)

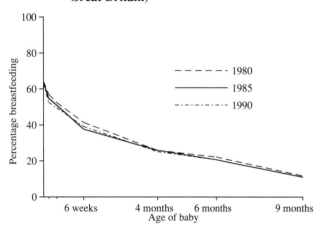

Figure 2.8   Prevalence of breastfeeding at ages up to nine months by country - England and Wales and in Scotland (1980, 1985 and 1990)

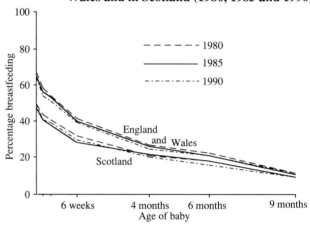

1985 and 1990, mothers could have stopped breastfeeding at different times, resulting in differences in prevalence of breastfeeding among older babies.

However, except for a slight fall in the percentage breastfeeding at one week (55% in 1985 compared with 53% in 1990), there has been virtually no change in the prevalence of breastfeeding in Great Britain as a whole at ages up to nine months (Table 2.27 and Figure 2.7). The separate rates for England and Wales and Scotland also show no change (Table 2.27 and Figure 2.8).

As in previous years the 1990 rates for Scotland were substantially lower than for England and Wales at all ages.

Since 1974 there has been an officially endorsed recommendation that mothers breastfeed their babies, preferably for four to six months, but at least for the first few weeks of life. The 1990 prevalence figures show that mothers in Great Britain are nowhere near achieving this aim. In 1990, only half the mothers (50%) breastfed even for as long as two weeks and only a quarter (25%) breastfed for four months or more.

Since the prevalence of breastfeeding at ages such as six weeks or four months depends significantly on the proportion of mothers who started breastfeeding, it is not surprising to find a similar pattern of differences between different subgroups to those for the incidence of breastfeeding already presented. The 1980, 1985 and 1990 prevalence rates for the main

Table 2.28   Estimated prevalence of breastfeeding at six weeks by birth order, standardised for social class as defined by current or last occupation of husband/partner, mother's education and region, compared with the unstandardised rate (1990 Great Britain)

Birth order	Standardised	Unstandardised
	Percentage who breastfed initially	
First births	38	39
Later births	38	38

Table 2.29   Estimated prevalence of breastfeeding at six weeks by social class as defined by current or last occupation of husband/partner, standardised for birth order, mother's education and region, compared with the unstandardised rate (1990 Great Britain)

Social class	Standardised	Unstandardised
	Percentage who breastfed initially	
I	57	68
II	49	56
IIINM	44	47
IIIM	36	33
IV and V	30	26
Unclassified and no partner	28	25

subgroups looked at in this study are presented in Tables 2.50 to 2.54 at the end of the chapter, but will not be commented on in detail.

Table 2.30 Estimated prevalence of breastfeeding at six weeks by mother's education, standardised for birth order, social class as defined by current or last occupation of husband/partner, and region, as compared with the unstandardised rate (1990 Great Britain)

Mother's age at finishing full-time education	Standardised	Unstandardised
	Percentage who breastfed initially	
16 or under	28	26
17 or 18	43	45
Over 18	63	71

Table 2.31 Estimated prevalence of breastfeeding at six weeks by region, standardised for birth order, social class as defined by current or last occupation of husband/partner and mother's education, compared with the unstandardised rate (1990 Great Britain)

Region	Standardised	Unstandardised
	Percentage who breastfed initially	
London and South East	45	49
South West and Wales	44	45
Midlands and East Anglia	36	33
North	32	29
Scotland	30	30

A similar analysis to that described in Section 2.1.11 using the maximum likelihood procedure was carried out to produce standardised prevalence rates at six weeks for birth order, social class, mother's education and region. These results are shown in Tables 2.28 to 2.31. The standardised prevalence figures at six weeks for first and later births are largely similar to the unstandardised rates but for the other variables standardisation has reduced the range of results found in the different subgroups. Despite this reduction, the standardised rates are still significantly different for each subgroup; the only exceptions being birth order and the difference between London and the South East and South West and Wales. This indicates that although some of the apparent differences between subgroups were due to interrelationships between the variables, social class, mother's education level and region were independently related to the prevalence of breastfeeding.

2.3 Duration of breastfeeding

In order to separate out the effect of differences in the incidence of breastfeeding from differences in the length of time for which mothers who breastfeed continue to do so, it is necessary to look separately at those mothers who began breastfeeding. The results presented in this section relate only to mothers who started breastfeeding at all, and show how long they continued breastfeeding, even if they were also giving other foods.

Between 1985 and 1990 there has been no change in the length of time for which mothers breastfeed for Great Britain as a whole, or for England and Wales (Table 2.32 and Figure 2.9). The situation in Scotland was very similar to that in 1985 except that fewer mothers breastfed for as long as four months; 39% in 1990 compared with 45% in 1985.

Figure 2.9 Duration of breastfeeding for those who were breast fed initially (1980,1985 and 1990 Great Britain)

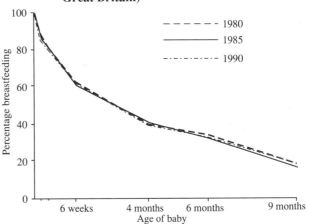

Table 2.32 Duration of breastfeeding for those who were breastfed initially by country (1980, 1985 and 1990)

	England and Wales			Scotland*			Great Britain		
	1980	1985	1990	1980	1985	1990	1980	1985	1990
	Percentage still breastfeeding								
Birth	100	100	100	100	100	100	100	100	100
1 week	88	87	85	89	85	83	88	86	85
2 weeks	81	81	80	81	79	77	81	81	80
6 weeks	63	61	62	64	60	60	63	61	62
4 months	40	40	39	42	45	39	40	41	39
6 months	34	33	33	36	36	33	34	33	33
9 months	18	17	18	18	20	19	18	17	18
Base:	*2,499*	*3,052*	*3,159*	*861*	*918*	*994*	*2,734*	*3,319*	*3,395*

* *The data for Scotland are weighted to give a national estimate.*

The duration of breastfeeding during the first eight weeks has been examined in more detail in 1990 to find out if the rate of breastfeeding declined steadily, or whether there were particular points in time where it fell sharply. Table 2.33 shows the rate at which breastfeeding mothers stopped breastfeeding in the first eight weeks. The table shows that for Great Britain as a whole, a distinctly large proportion of mothers (15%) who started breastfeeding stopped doing so during the first week. Then around 5% of the mothers stopped each week between the second and fifth week. The decline then slowed to 2% in the sixth week, increased to 5% in the seventh week to slow down to 2% again in the eighth week. Thus after a sharp drop at the first week the proportion of mothers who breastfed fell at a steady rate in the first 8 weeks. This pattern is evident in England and Wales and in Scotland, as well as within the main subgroups in the study.

Table 2.33   The rate at which breastfeeding mothers stopped breastfeeding in the first eight weeks by country (1990)

	England and Wales	Scotland*	Great Britain
	Percentage stopping breastfeeding		
During the first week	15	17	15
During the second week	5	6	5
During the third week	6	5	6
During the fourth week	5	5	5
During the fifth week	5	4	5
During the sixth week	2	3	2
During the seventh week	5	3	5
During the eighth week	2	2	2
Base:	*3,159*	*994*	*3,395*

* The data for Scotland are weighted to give a national estimate.

Table 2.34   Duration of breastfeeding for those who were breastfed initially for first and later births (1980, 1985 and 1990 Great Britain)

	First births			Later births			All babies*		
	1980	1985	1990	1980	1985	1990	1980	1985	1990
	Percentage still breastfeeding								
Birth	100	100	100	100	100	100	100	100	100
1 week	85	83	82	90	90	87	88	86	85
2 weeks	78	76	76	84	85	83	81	81	80
6 weeks	59	56	57	67	65	66	63	61	62
4 months	35	36	34	45	46	45	40	41	39
6 months	29	28	27	39	38	39	34	33	33
9 months	14	14	14	22	21	23	18	17	18
Base:	*1,349*	*1,642*	*1,620*	*1,377*	*1,677*	*1,725*	*2,734*	*3,319*	*3,395*

* Includes some cases for whom birth order was not known.

Table 2.35   Duration of breastfeeding for those who were breastfed initially by social class as defined by current or last occupation of husband/partner (1980, 1985 and 1990 Great Britain)

	Social class											
	I			II			IINM			IIIM		
	1980	1985	1990	1980	1985	1990	1980	1985	1990	1980	1985	1990
	Percentage still breastfeeding											
Birth	100	100	100	100	100	100	100	100	100	100	100	100
1 week	94	95	94	91	91	89	85	88	86	86	84	82
2 weeks	91	91	90	87	86	85	80	82	82	79	79	76
6 weeks	85	81	78	74	72	71	62	61	65	56	56	57
4 months	67	62	56	53	54	50	39	40	38	32	36	34
6 months	57	52	46	46	45	43	34	33	30	27	27	28
9 months	36	27	27	22	26	23	18	15	18	13	14	16
Base:	*293*	*268*	*343*	*601*	*830*	*833*	*273*	*332*	*311*	*1,051*	*1,009*	*951*

	IV			V			No partner			Unclassified		
	1980	1985	1990	1980	1985	1990	1980	1985	1990	1980	1985	1990
	Percentage still breastfeeding											
Birth	..	100	100	..	100	100	..	100	100	..	100	100
1 week	..	82	80	..	85	80	..	77	77	..	85	90
2 weeks	..	74	73	..	76	73	..	69	71	..	79	85
6 weeks	..	51	51	..	46	51	..	43	45	..	56	67
4 months	..	29	31	..	22	26	..	22	23	..	39	41
6 months	..	22	28	..	17	23	..	18	17	..	36	36
9 months	..	9	15	..	6	11	..	11	9	..	25	19
Base:	*..*	*425*	*393*	*..*	*107*	*47*	*..*	*235*	*326*	*..*	*114*	*190*

.. 1980 data not available.

2.3.1 Duration of breastfeeding and birth order

Table 2.34 shows that there was no change in the duration of breastfeeding among mothers of first babies between 1985 and 1990. However, slightly fewer mothers having a second or subsequent baby breastfed for at least a week (87% in 1990 compared with 90% in 1985). In 1980 and 1985 it had been found that mothers who had previous children were more likely to continue breastfeeding up to the age of nine months. This was also true in 1990, where 23% of mothers of second or subsequent children breastfed for at least nine months, compared with 14% of mothers of first births.

2.3.2 Duration of breastfeeding and social class (as defined by current or last occupation of mother's husband/partner)

The figures for the duration of breastfeeding for mothers in each of the social class groups have shown little change over time (Table 2.35). However, comparing the 1985 and 1990 figures shows that in 1990 there was a tendency for mothers in Social Class I and II to be less likely to breastfeed for as long as four months whereas mothers in Social Class IV and V were more likely than previously to breastfeed for periods of six months or more. In 1990, 56% of mothers in Social Class I breastfed for four months or more; a decline from 62% in 1985. Twenty-eight per cent of mothers in Social Class IV breastfed for six months or more in 1990: an increase from 22% in 1985.

Mothers whose social class could not be classified were more likely than they had been in 1985 to breastfeed for periods up to six weeks; 67% were breastfeeding for at least six weeks in 1990 compared with 56% in 1985.

The regular pattern of a shorter duration of breastfeeding in each consecutively lower social class group found in previous surveys was also apparent in 1990. The proportion of mothers still breastfeeding when their babies were 4 months old illustrates this and is presented in Figure 2.10. As in 1985, mothers with no partner were the most likely to give up breastfeeding after only a few weeks. Only 45% of them were still breastfeeding when their baby was six weeks old, compared with 78% of mothers in Social Class I (Table 2.35).

2.3.3 Duration of breastfeeding and age at which mother completed full-time education

Table 2.36 shows that in 1990, as in previous years, duration of breastfeeding is longest among mothers who finished full-time education after the age of 18 years, and shortest among those who finished at age 16 years or below. Compared with 1985 there has been no change in the duration of breastfeeding among mothers who left school at 16 years or below. A slightly smaller proportion of mothers who left full-time education between the age of 17 and 18 years breastfed for at least a week (86% in 1990 compared with 89% in 1985). But the most notable change was among those who breastfed for longest, mothers who left full-time education after 18 years were not breastfeeding for as long as they had done in 1985. Table 2.23 shows that 59% of these mothers breastfed for at least four months in 1990 compared with 66% in 1985, and the proportions still breastfeeding at six months and nine months have also decreased. Despite this decline mothers who left full-time education after the age of 18 years were nevertheless twice as likely to breastfeed for at least four months in 1990 compared with those who left school aged 16 or under.

Figure 2.10 Proportion of mothers still breastfeeding at four months by social class as defined by current or last occupation of husband/partner (1980, 1985 and 1990 Great Britain)

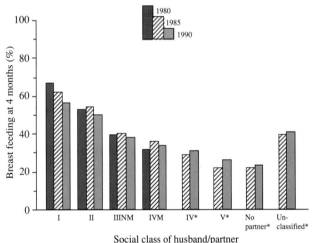

* 1980 figures for Social class IV & V, no partner and unclassified not available.

Table 2.36 Duration of breastfeeding for those who were breastfed initially by age at which mother finished full-time education (1980, 1985 and 1990 Great Britain)

| | Age at which mother finished full-time education | | | | | | | | | | | |
| | 16 or under | | | 17 or 18 | | | Over 18 | | | All babies* | | |
	1980	1985	1990	1980	1985	1990	1980	1985	1990	1980	1985	1990
	Percentage still breastfeeding											
Birth	100	100	100	100	100	100	100	100	100	100	100	100
1 week	84	82	80	90	89	86	94	95	93	88	86	85
2 weeks	76	75	74	83	83	81	91	91	90	81	81	80
6 weeks	54	50	52	65	64	63	84	81	79	63	61	62
4 months	29	30	28	43	40	42	66	66	59	40	41	39
6 months	25	24	24	34	32	34	57	56	49	34	33	33
9 months	12	12	13	19	17	19	32	31	28	18	17	18
Base:	*1,450*	*1,633*	*1,446*	*675*	*1,013*	*1,217*	*584*	*647*	*702*	*2,734*	*3,319*	*3,395*

* Includes some cases where mother's education was not known.

Table 2.37   Duration of breastfeeding at ages up to nine months by sex of baby by country (1990)

	England and Wales		Scotland*		Great Britain	
	Boys	Girls	Boys	Girls	Boys	Girls
	Percentage still breastfeeding					
Birth	100	100	100	100	100	100
1 week	85	86	82	83	84	86
2 weeks	79	81	76	78	79	81
6 weeks	61	63	56	63	61	63
4 months	39	40	38	41	39	40
6 months	33	33	31	35	33	33
9 months	19	18	16	22	18	19
Base:	*1,621*	*1,535*	*448*	*507*	*1,738*	*1,657*

* The data for Scotland are weighted to give a national estimate.

Table 2.38   Duration of breastfeeding for those who were breastfed initially by region (1980, 1985 and 1990)

	London and South East			South West and Wales			Midlands and East Anglia			North			Scotland*		
	1980	1985	1990	1980	1985	1990	1980	1985	1990	1980	1985	1990	1980	1985	1990
	Percentage still breastfeeding														
Birth	100	100	100	100	100	100	100	100	100	100	100	100	100	100	100
1 week	88	89	88	91	88	89	86	86	83	87	82	80	89	85	83
2 weeks	82	84	83	84	82	85	79	80	77	80	76	75	81	79	77
6 weeks	67	64	67	67	69	70	56	57	56	60	54	54	64	60	60
4 months	43	43	43	40	49	49	37	38	35	39	32	33	42	45	39
6 months	36	36	35	34	40	43	33	30	30	31	26	27	36	36	33
9 months	20	18	18	16	22	24	17	13	17	17	16	17	18	20	19
Base:	*974*	*1,241*	*1,320*	*316*	*449*	*432*	*512*	*595*	*610*	*696*	*766*	*797*	*861*	*918*	*994*

* The data for Scotland are weighted to give a national estimate.

2.3.4   Duration of breastfeeding and sex of baby

It was mentioned earlier that mothers who had baby girls were just as likely to start breastfeeding as mothers with baby boys in 1990. Table 2.37 shows that in England and Wales and in Great Britain as a whole, mothers were just as likely to breastfeed a baby girl for as long as they would breastfeed a baby boy. However this was not the case among mothers in Scotland. These mothers were more likely to breastfeed a baby girl than a boy for periods of six weeks or longer. Sixty-three per cent of baby girls were breastfed for at least six weeks compared with 56% of baby boys, and 22% of baby girls were breastfed for at least nine months compared with 16% of baby boys. Figures on the prevalence of breastfeeding by the sex of the baby presented in Table 2.53 also show that in Scotland baby girls were more likely than baby boys to be breastfed after six weeks.

2.3.5   Duration of breastfeeding and region

The 1985 survey revealed a regional effect on the duration of breastfeeding, with duration decreasing from south to north in England and Wales. Table 2.38 and Figure 2.11 show that this regional pattern was still apparent in 1990. In 1990, as in 1985, duration rates in Scotland did not fit neatly into this 'north/south' picture. The Scottish rates were again higher than those in the northern regions of England and Wales but lower than those in the southern regions.

Figure 2.11   Duration of breastfeeding for those who were breastfed initially by region (1990)

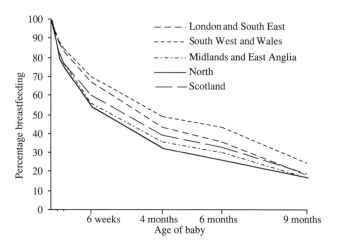

It was mentioned earlier that a smaller proportion of mothers in the Midlands and East Anglia, and in the South West and Wales started breastfeeding. This slight decline in the incidence of breastfeeding was not accompanied by a decrease in the duration of breastfeeding in these regions. No change has been detected in the duration of breastfeeding in any of the four regions in England and Wales; mothers in 1990 were breastfeeding for as long as their counterparts in 1985 (Table 2.38).

The situation in Scotland was slightly different. Table 2.38 shows that fewer mothers in Scotland were breastfeeding for as long as four months in 1990 compared with 1985, 39% compared with 45%. There has also been a slight decline in the proportion breastfeeding for at least six months.

2.3.6 Duration of breastfeeding and previous experience of feeding a baby

It was pointed out earlier that previous experience of feeding affects whether a mother starts breastfeeding. Table 2.39 shows that previous experience also has an effect on how long a mother continues to breastfeed. In 1990, as in 1985, only a minority of mothers breastfed a later child without having previously breastfed, and those who did so were much less successful than those with previous experience of breastfeeding. In 1990, 70% of women with previous experience of breastfeeding breastfed for at least six weeks compared with only 31% of those with no experience of breastfeeding. By the time their baby was nine months old, 25% of mothers with previous experience of breastfeeding were still breastfeeding compared with only 8% of mothers with no previous breastfeeding experience.

However, in 1990 women with no previous experience of breastfeeding stopped after a shorter period of time than their counterparts in 1985 and 1980; in 1990, 31% of the mothers with no previous breastfeeding experience were still breastfeeding at six weeks, compared with 43% in 1985 and 49% in 1980. In contrast, women who had breastfed an earlier baby were breastfeeding their current baby for as long as their counterparts in 1985 and 1980. The report of the 1985 survey[3] called for more help and support in breastfeeding for mothers with no previous experience in breastfeeding. The 1990 results have identified an even greater need to support mothers with no previous breastfeeding experience if the decline in the duration of breastfeeding among this group is to be halted.

2.3.7 Duration of breastfeeding and smoking

As well as mothers who smoked (either before or during pregnancy) being less likely to have breastfed their baby in the first place in 1990, Table 2.40 shows that those that did were

Table 2.40 Duration of breastfeeding by whether mother smoked during pregnancy or not (1985 and 1990, Great Britain)

	Non-smoker		Smoker	
	1985	1990	1985	1990
	Percentage still breastfeeding			
Birth	100	100	100	100
1 week	88	87	79	78
2 weeks	83	82	73	72
6 weeks	65	65	46	47
4 months	45	43	24	25
6 months	36	36	19	19
9 months	19	20	10	10
Base:	*2,605*	*2,708*	*714*	*687*

more likely to stop after shorter periods of time than mothers who did not smoke. This had also been the case in 1985. Only 25% of mothers who smoked during pregnancy continued breastfeeding for as long as four months compared with 43% of those who did not smoke during pregnancy in 1990. As Table 2.41 showed, this was not due to the relationship between smoking and social class; within each social class group smokers gave up breastfeeding sooner than non-smokers. Between 1985 and 1990 there has been very little change in the duration of breastfeeding according to mother's smoking behaviour.

2.3.8 Duration of breastfeeding and drinking alcohol

Table 2.42 presents the length of time for which women who drank alcohol during pregnancy and those who abstained from alcohol breastfed their baby in 1990. As in the analysis of the incidence of breastfeeding and drinking, the women in the sample have been divided into three groups, namely drinkers, light drinkers and non-drinkers. Light drinkers are women who drank less than one unit of alcohol a week during pregnancy and drinkers are women who drank one unit or more of alcohol a week during pregnancy. The last three columns of Table 2.42 show that drinkers and light drinkers were more likely than non-drinkers to breastfeed for between two weeks and four months; over 40% of drinkers and light drinkers breastfed for four months compared with 37% of non-drinkers. There was not much difference in the proportion of

Table 2.39 Duration of breastfeeding for those who were breastfed initially by mother's previous experience of breastfeeding (second and subsequent births only 1980, 1985 and 1990)

	No experience of breastfeeding			Experience of breastfeeding			All second and subsequent babies*		
	1980	1985	1990	1980	1985	1990	1980	1985	1990
	Percentage still breastfeeding								
Birth	100	100	100	100	100	100	100	100	100
1 week	75	74	62	93	92	91	90	90	88
2 weeks	65	63	56	87	87	87	84	85	84
6 weeks	49	43	31	70	68	70	67	65	66
4 months	27	20	15	47	48	49	45	46	45
6 months	23	14	11	41	40	42	39	38	39
9 months	13	6	8	23	22	25	22	21	23
Base:	*207*	*157*	*159*	*1,169*	*1,498*	*1,492*	*1,377*	*1,677*	*1,725*

* The data for Scotland are weighted to give a national estimate.

Table 2.41 Duration of breastfeeding by whether mother smoked during pregnancy and social class as defined by current or last occupation of husband/partner (1985 and 1990 Great Britain)

	Social class											
	I and II				IIINM				IIIM			
	Non-smoker		Smoker		Non-smoker		Smoker		Non-smoker		Smoker	
	1985	1990	1985	1990	1985	1990	1985	1990	1985	1990	1985	1990
	Percentage still breastfeeding											
Birth	100	100	100	100	100	100	100	100	100	100	100	100
1 week	92	91	88	87	87	87	93	81	86	84	79	76
2 weeks	88	87	81	81	81	82	85	80	81	78	75	69
6 weeks	76	75	66	55	61	65	60	59	60	60	45	47
4 months	58	54	36	34	40	43	39	24	40	39	23	25
6 months	49	46	26	25	34	32	23	20	30	30	18	19
9 months	27	25	15	12	16	18	6	15	15	18	10	10
Base:	*961*	*1,056*	*136*	*121*	*284*	*267*	*48*	*44*	*754*	*730*	*254*	*221*

	IV				V				Unclassified and no partner			
	Non-smoker		Smoker		Non-smoker		Smoker		Non-smoker		Smoker	
	1985	1990	1985	1990	1985	1990	1985	1990	1985	1990	1985	1990
	Percentage still breastfeeding											
Birth	100	100	100	100	100	100	100	100	100	100	100	100
1 week	85	80	74	78	89	82	77	74	86	85	71	75
2 weeks	77	73	66	75	81	79	69	58	79	80	63	70
6 weeks	54	51	40	49	51	54	36	44	55	61	29	37
4 months	31	34	21	25	26	31	16	16	31	35	10	20
6 months	23	31	17	20	21	28	8	10	23	29	9	15
9 months	9	17	11	12	8	15	1	1	16	16	6	8
Base:	*321*	*290*	*105*	*102*	*66*	*34*	*40*	*14*	*219*	*331*	*130*	*185*

.. 1980 data not available.

Table 2.42 Duration of breastfeeding by whether mother drank alcohol during pregnancy or not and social class as defined by current or last occupation of husband/partner (1990 Great Britain)

	Social class								
	I and II			IIINM			IIIM		
	Non-drinker	Light drinker*	Drinker†	Non-drinker	Light drinker*	Drinker†	Non-drinker	Light drinker*	Drinker†
	Percentage still breastfeeding								
Birth	100	100	100	100	100	100	100	100	100
1 week	89	91	93	82	87	91	80	82	84
2 weeks	82	87	90	77	82	88	75	75	80
6 weeks	68	74	79	63	64	69	53	57	63
4 months	47	53	56	40	40	31	33	33	38
6 months	41	46	43	33	32	18	26	27	32
9 months	27	23	23	17	18	15	18	15	19
Base:	*334*	*624*	*218*	*100*	*151*	*60*	*294*	*468*	*189*

	IV			V, unclassified and no partner			All mothers		
	Non-drinker	Light drinker*	Drinker†	Non-drinker	Light drinker*	Drinker†	Non-drinker	Light drinker*	Drinker†
	Percentage still breastfeeding								
Birth	100	100	100	100	100	100	100	100	100
1 week	75	82	81	85	80	79	83	86	86
2 weeks	68	76	79	77	76	72	77	80	82
6 weeks	48	48	62	55	54	44	58	62	65
4 months	26	31	40	31	32	22	37	41	40
6 months	26	29	29	26	25	18	32	34	31
9 months	13	15	21	16	11	12	20	18	19
Base:	*137*	*184*	*73*	*208*	*235*	*122*	*1,074*	*1,660*	*661*

* Light drinkers are defined as women who drank less than one unit of alcohol a week during pregnancy.
† Drinkers are defined as women who drank one unit or more of alcohol a week during pregnancy.

drinkers, light drinkers and non-drinkers who breastfed for one week, six months or nine months.

The national pattern above was also apparent in Social Classes I and II but it was not replicated in the other social class groups. Table 2.42 shows that drinkers, light drinkers and non-drinkers in Social Class III non-manual were just as likely to breastfeed up to four months but a smaller proportion of drinkers breastfed for as long as six months (18% of drinkers compared with between 32% and 33% of light and non-drinkers). Drinkers and light drinkers in Social Class III manual were more likely to breastfeed for between two months and six weeks. Drinkers in Social Class IV were more likely to breastfeed for between six weeks to four months than their non-drinking peers (40% of drinkers in Social Class IV breastfed for four months compared with between 26% and 31% of non-drinkers and light drinkers). In contrast, drinkers in Social Class V, women not living with a husband/partner, and those whose social class could not be classified were less likely to breastfeed for between six weeks to six months; 22% of drinkers in this group breastfed for four months compared with between 31% and 32% of non-drinkers and light drinkers.

2.3.9 Duration of breastfeeding and mother's employment status

Mothers were classified into one of the following five groups according to their working status during the first nine months of their baby's life:

(i)   those who were working when the baby was about six weeks old and continued working throughout the rest of the nine months ('working all the time' in Table 2.43);

(ii)   those that returned to work when the baby was between six weeks and four months old ('went back to work by four months');

(iii)   those that returned to work when the baby was between four months and nine months old ('went back to work by nine months');

(iv)   those that did not work at all during the first nine months ('not working any of the time');

(v)   those whose pattern of work followed some other arrangement ('others').

Table 2.43 and Figure 2.12 show that in 1990, as in 1985, the duration of breastfeeding was similar for all these groups of mothers regardless of their working status. There was virtually no difference in the duration of breastfeeding between mothers who did not work at all during the first nine months and those who worked throughout this period. Returning to work did seem to reduce slightly the length of time for which mothers continued to breastfeed. For example, 31% of mothers who went back to work when their baby was aged between six weeks and four months were still breastfeeding when the baby was four months old, compared with 42% of mothers who did not work at all during the first nine months, and 48% of mothers who did not go back to work until after the baby was four months old.

The relationship between duration of breastfeeding and mother's working status has changed little between 1985 and 1990. The only notable difference was that a higher proportion of mothers who went back to work between four and nine months

Figure 2.12 Duration of breastfeeding for those who were breastfed initially by mother's working status (1990, Great Britain)

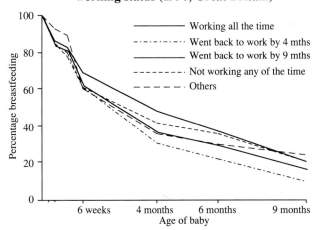

Table 2.43   Duration of breastfeeding by mother's working status during the first nine months (1985 and 1990 Great Britain)

	Working all the time		Went back to work by four months		Went back to work by nine months		Not working any of the time		Others	
	1985	1990	1985	1990	1985	1990	1985	1990	1985	1990
	Percentage still breastfeeding									
Birth	100	100	100	100	100	100	100	100	100	100
1 week	87	84	88	85	91	86	86	85	90	93
2 weeks	82	81	82	78	87	83	80	80	85	89
6 weeks	60	63	59	61	67	69	61	61	68	60
4 months	41	37	34	31	46	48	41	42	54	36
6 months	33	30	22	22	34	37	34	36	44	30
9 months	17	17	12	10	14	21	18	20	18	24
Base:	*121*	*179*	*266*	*561*	*406*	*580*	*2,438*	*1,898*	*90*	*73*

in 1990 were still breastfeeding when their baby was nine months old (21% in 1990 compared with 14% in 1985).

It should be remembered, however, that a mother's working status is related to whether or not she is on maternity leave, which is in turn related to her social class, so it is very difficult to look at the effect of returning to work *per se*. This survey provides no evidence that returning to work significantly shortens the length of time for which a mother breastfeeds.

2.3.10 *Estimating the separate effects on the duration of breastfeeding*

The figures for the duration of breastfeeding set out in the previous tables are, like those for the incidence and prevalence of breastfeeding presented earlier, affected by interrelationships between different variables. A similar maximum likelihood procedure was therefore carried out to estimate the proportion of babies breastfed initially who were still being breastfed at six weeks, controlling for these interrelationships. The results are presented in Tables 2.44 to 2.48.

The estimates set out in Table 2.44 show that the group estimated to have the largest proportion still breastfeeding at six weeks would be mothers having their second or subsequent babies who were educated beyond the age of eighteen years, whose husband had professional or managerial occupations (Social Class I) and whose babies were born in the South West

and Wales. This was also the case in 1985. The estimated proportion still breastfeeding at six weeks for this group was 91% in 1990. At the other extreme, the group estimated to have the smallest proportion still breastfeeding at six weeks would be mothers of first babies who left school aged 16 years or under, whose husband were in semi-skilled or unskilled occupations (Social Classes IV and V) and whose babies were born in the north of England.

Tables 2.45 to 2.48 show the proportion still breastfeeding at six weeks for each of the four main variables in the analysis (birth order, social class, mother's education level and region) standardised for the interrelationship between the four variables. The standardised proportion still breastfeeding at six weeks for first and later births are largely similar to the unstandardised rates, but for the other three variables standardisation has reduced the range of results found in the different subgroups. Despite this reduction, the standardised rates are still significantly different for each subgroup; the only exception being the difference between Social Classes IV and V and mothers with no partner or whose social class could not be classified. This indicates that although some of the apparent differences between subgroups were due to interrelationships between the variables, all four variables (birth order, social class, mother's eduction level and region) were independently related to the proportion still breastfeeding at six weeks in 1990 as in 1985.

Table 2.44   Estimated proportion breastfed at six weeks of those who were breastfed initially (1990 Great Britain)

Birth order	Mothers age at finishing full-time education	Region	Social class					
			I	II	IIINM	IIIM	IV & V	Unclassified
			Percentage who breast fed initially					
First births	16 or under	London & SE	65	58	54	48	43	43
		SW & Wales	70	63	59	54	49	49
		Midlands	59	52	48	43	37	38
		North	56	48	44	39	34	35
		Scotland	59	51	47	42	37	37
	17 or 18	London & SE	73	67	63	58	52	53
		SW & Wales	78	72	68	64	58	59
		Midlands	68	61	57	52	47	47
		North	66	58	54	49	43	44
		Scotland	68	61	56	52	46	47
	Over 18	London & SE	84	79	76	72	67	68
		SW & Wales	87	83	80	77	72	73
		Midlands	80	75	72	67	62	63
		North	79	72	69	64	59	60
		Scotland	80	74	71	67	62	62
Later births	16 or under	London & SE	73	67	63	58	52	53
		SW & Wales	78	71	68	64	58	59
		Midlands	68	61	57	52	47	47
		North	65	58	54	49	43	43
		Scotland	68	61	57	52	46	47
	17 or 18	London & SE	80	75	71	67	62	63
		SW & Wales	84	79	76	72	67	68
		Midlands	76	70	66	62	56	57
		North	74	67	63	59	53	54
		Scotland	76	69	66	61	56	56
	Over 18	London & SE	88	85	82	79	75	76
		SW & Wales	91	87	86	83	79	80
		Midlands	86	81	79	75	71	71
		North	84	79	76	73	68	68
		Scotland	85	81	78	75	70	71

Table 2.45 Estimated proportion breastfed at six weeks of those who were breastfed initially by birth order, standardised for social class as defined by current or last occupation of husband/partner, mother's education and region, compared with the unstandardised rate (1990 Great Britain)

Birth order	Standardised	Unstandardised
	Percentage still breastfeeding at six weeks	
First births	57	57
Later births	65	66

Table 2.46 Estimated proportion breastfed at six weeks of those who were breastfed initially by social class as defined by current or last occupation of husband/partner standardised for birth order, mother's education and region, compared with the unstandardised rate (1990 Great Britain)

Social class	Standardised	Unstandardised
	Percentage still breastfeeding at six weeks	
I	73	78
II	67	71
IIINM	63	65
IIIM	59	57
IV and V	53	51
Unclassified and no partner	54	53

Table 2.47 Estimated proportion breastfed at six weeks of those who were breastfed initially by mother's education, standardised for birth order, social class as defined by current or last occupation of husband/partner and region, compared with the unstandardised rate (1990 Great Britain)

Mother's age at finishing full-time education	Standardised	Unstandardised
	Percentage still breastfeeding at six weeks	
16 or under	53	52
17 or 18	62	63
Over 18	75	79

Table 2.48 Estimated proportion breastfed at six weeks of those who were breastfed initially by region, standardised for birth order, social class as defined by current or last occupation of husband/partner, mother's education and region, compared with the unstandardised rate (1990 Great Britain)

Region	Standardised	Unstandardised
	Percentage still breastfeeding at six weeks	
London and South East	64	67
South West and Wales	68	70
Midlands and East Anglia	58	56
North	55	54
Scotland	58	60

2.3.11 The characteristics of mothers who breastfed for different lengths of time in the first nine months

The previous section and section 2.1.11 show that, in 1990 as well as in 1985, whether a mother ever breastfed her baby and the length of time for which she breastfed were related to socio-demographic variables such as birth order, social class and education level. It is therefore of interest to assess whether mothers who breastfed for different lengths of time had particular characteristics. If so, the information can be used to identify specific groups of mothers who are most likely not to breastfeed or to stop breastfeeding at a particular period in the first nine months.

To examine the characteristics of mothers who breast fed for different lengths of time Table 2.49 groups the mothers in the sample according to whether they ever breastfed and if they had breastfed, the time at which they stopped doing so. Mothers who bottle fed from birth in 1990 tended to be mothers having their second or subsequent baby. They were also more likely to have left full-time education at the age of 16 years or under. In terms of social class, mothers who bottle fed from birth were more likely to be from Social Classes III, IV and V, or not living with a partner or whose social class was unclassified. The first column of Table 2.49 shows that, in 1990, 62% of the mothers who bottle fed from birth were mothers of a second or subsequent baby, 72% of these mothers left full-time education at the age of 16 years or under, 39% of this group were from Social Class III, and 48% of them were from Social Classes IV and V or not living with a partner or whose social class was unclassified.

Mothers who stopped breastfeeding before their baby was one week old and those who stopped when their baby was between one and two weeks old had similar characteristics and are thus grouped together for examination. The second column of Table 2.49 indicates that mothers who stopped breastfeeding before their baby was two weeks old were marginally more likely to be mothers having their first baby (58% were mothers of a first baby). The majority of these mothers left full-time education before the age of 19 years (55% left full-time education aged 16 years or under and 34% left full-time education between the age of 17 and 18 years). Similar to mothers who bottle fed from birth, the mothers who breastfed for less than two weeks tended to be from the lower social class groups; 42% of these mothers were from Social Class III and 35% were from Social Classes IV and V or not living with a partner or whose social class was unclassified.

Mothers who stopped breastfeeding when their baby was between two weeks but less than six weeks old also tended to be from the lower social class groups and to have left full-time education before the age of 19 years. In 1990, 39% of these mothers were from Social Class III and 36% were from Social Classes IV and V or not living with a partner or whose social class was unclassified (third column of Table 2.49). Over half of these mothers (52%) left full-time education at the age of 16 years or under and 35% left education between the ages of 17 and 18 years.

The mothers who gave up breastfeeding when their baby was six weeks but less than four months old again tended to have left full-time education before the age of 19 years. The fourth column of Table 2.49 shows that 46% of these mothers left

Table 2.49 Selected characteristics of mothers in the sample by the time at which they stopped breastfeeding (1990 Great Britain)

Selected characteristics of mother	Time at which mother stopped breastfeeding							All mothers in the sample
	Bottle feeding from birth	Stopped in first two weeks	Stopped between two weeks but less than six weeks	Stopped between six weeks but less than four months	Stopped between four months but less than six months	Stopped between six months but less than nine months	Breastfeeding for nine months or more	
	%	%	%	%	%	%	%	%
Birth order of baby								
First birth	38	58	52	52	52	44	38	45
Second or subsequent birth	62	42	48	48	48	56	62	55
Social class as defined by current or last occupation of husband/partner								
I and II	14	24	26	32	39	48	45	27
IIINM and IIIM	39	42	39	40	36	30	34	38
IV, V, no partner and unclassified	48	35	36	28	25	22	21	35
Age at which mother completed full-time education								
16 or under	72	55	52	46	28	31	30	54
17-18	25	34	35	36	41	38	38	32
Over 18	4	11	13	19	30	31	31	14
Base:	2,018*†	681*†	605*†	738*†	242*†	465*†	589*†	5,413*†

* *Excludes some cases where duration of breastfeeding was not known.*
† *Includes some cases where the age at which mother completed full-time education was not known.*

full-time education at the age of 16 years or under, and 36% left education between the age of 17 and 18 years. At this stage mothers from Social Class III were the most likely to stop breastfeeding. Just over 40% of the mothers who stopped breastfeeding between six weeks and four months were from Social Class III compared with 32% from Social Classes I and II and 28% from Social Classes IV and V or not living with a partner or whose social class was unclassified.

The results so far indicate that women who stopped breastfeeding before their baby was four months old tended to be from the lower social class groups. Thus, by the time the baby was four months old, over 50% of mothers in Social Classes I and II who ever breast fed were still breastfeeding, compared with between 23% to 38% among mothers from the other social class groups (Table 2.35). As the majority of mothers in the lower social class groups had stopped breastfeeding before their baby was four months old, the mothers who stopped breastfeeding when their baby was four months but less than six months old were slightly more likely to be from Social Classes I and II. The fifth column of Table 2.49 shows that 39% of those who stopped breastfeeding at this stage were from Social Classes I and II, while mothers from the other social class groups accounted for between 25% to 36% of the mothers who stopped breastfeeding between four to six months. In terms of educational level, mothers who stopped breastfeeding when their baby was between four and six months were most likely to have left full-time education between the age of 17 and 18 years; 41% compared with 30% among those who left full-time education aged 19 years and over and 28% among those who left education aged 16 years or under.

Mothers who gave up breastfeeding when their babies were six but less than nine months old were also the most likely to be in Social Classes I and II (48%) because most of the mothers in the other social class groups had given up breastfeeding (sixth column of Table 2.49). Mothers who stopped breastfeeding at this stage were also slightly more likely to have left full-time education between the age of 17 and 18 years; 38% compared with 31% among mothers who left education at the other ages. In addition, mothers who gave up breastfeeding at this stage tended to be mothers of second or subsequent babies (56% compared with 44% among mothers having their first baby).

This and various other sections of this chapter have revealed that mothers from the lower social class groups and who left school at the statutory school leaving age (16 years or under) were less likely to start breastfeeding and those who started breastfeeding were more likely to stop doing so after a short period. Thus mothers who breastfed for nine months or more tended to be from Social Classes I and II and to have left full-time education above the statutory school leaving age. The seventh column of Table 2.49 shows that 45% of the mothers who breastfed for nine months or more were from Social Classes I and II, 38% of them left full-time education between the age of 17 and 18 years, and 32% left education at 19 years and above. The mothers who breastfed for nine months or more were also more likely to be mothers of a second or subsequent baby (62%); this reflects the observation made earlier that mothers who had been successful in breastfeeding a previous baby tend to breastfeed and to continue breastfeeding for longer periods.

Table 2.50   Prevalence of breastfeeding at ages up to nine months for first and later births (1980, 1985 and 1990 Great Britain)

Age of baby	First births			Later births			All babies		
	1980	1985	1990	1980	1985	1990	1980	1985	1990
	Percentage breastfeeding at each age								
Birth	74	69	69	58	60	58	65	64	63
1 week	63	57	57	52	53	50	57	55	53
2 weeks	57	53	52	49	50	48	52	51	50
6 weeks	43	39	39	39	38	38	41	38	39
4 months	26	25	23	26	27	26	26	26	25
6 months	21	19	18	23	22	22	22	21	21
9 months	10	10	10	13	12	13	12	11	11
Base:	*1,831*	*2,347*	*2,430*	*2,377*	*2,875*	*2,983*	*4,224*	*5,223*	*5,413*

Table 2.51   Prevalence of breastfeeding at ages up to nine months by social class as defined by current or last occupation of husband/partner (1980, 1985 and 1990 Great Britain)

Age of baby	Social class											
	I			II			IIINM			IIIM		
	1980	1985	1990	1980	1985	1990	1980	1985	1990	1980	1985	1990
	Percentage breastfeeding at each age											
Birth	87	87	86	78	81	79	77	76	73	59	61	59
1 week	82	83	81	71	73	70	65	67	62	51	51	48
2 weeks	80	79	77	68	69	67	62	62	59	47	48	45
6 weeks	74	71	68	58	58	56	48	46	47	33	34	33
4 months	59	54	48	41	43	39	30	30	28	19	21	20
6 months	50	45	40	36	37	34	26	24	22	16	16	16
9 months	31	23	22	17	21	18	14	11	13	8	8	10
Base:	*335*	*307*	*398*	*769*	*1,028*	*1,052*	*335*	*436*	*427*	*1,769*	*1,666*	*1,611*

Age of baby	IV			V			No partner			Unclassified		
	1980	1985	1990	1980	1985	1990	1980	1985	1990	1980	1985	1990
	Percentage breastfeeding at each age											
Birth	..	58	53	..	43	41	..	55	61	..	39	43
1 week	..	47	42	..	36	32	..	46	54	..	30	33
2 weeks	..	43	39	..	33	29	..	43	51	..	27	30
6 weeks	..	29	27	..	20	20	..	30	40	..	16	19
4 months	..	16	16	..	9	10	..	20	25	..	8	10
6 months	..	12	15	..	7	9	..	19	22	..	6	7
9 months	..	5	8	..	2	4	..	13	11	..	4	4
Base:	*..*	*738*	*736*	*..*	*247*	*117*	*..*	*207*	*313*	*..*	*595*	*760*

.. Data not available.

Table 2.52   Prevalence of breastfeeding by age at which mother finished full-time education (1980, 1985 and 1990 Great Britain)

Age of baby	Age at which mother finished full-time education									All mothers*		
	16 or under			17 or 18			Over 18					
	1980	1985	1990	1980	1985	1990	1980	1985	1990	1980	1985	1990
	Percentage breastfeeding at each age											
Birth	55	53	50	76	75	71	89	89	91	65	64	63
1 week	46	43	40	68	66	61	84	85	84	57	55	53
2 weeks	42	39	37	63	63	57	81	82	81	52	51	50
6 weeks	30	26	26	49	48	45	75	73	71	41	38	39
4 months	16	15	14	33	30	30	59	59	53	26	26	25
6 months	14	12	12	26	24	24	51	50	44	22	21	21
9 months	7	6	7	14	13	14	28	28	25	12	11	11
Base:	*2,632*	*3,110*	*2,881*	*892*	*1,346*	*1,710*	*657*	*725*	*775*	*4,224*	*5,223*	*5,413*

* Includes some cases where mother's education was not known.

Table 2.53   Prevalence of breastfeeding at ages up to nine months by sex of baby by country (1990)

Age of baby	England and Wales		Scotland*		Great Britain	
	Boys	Girls	Boys	Girls	Boys	Girls
	Percentage still breastfeeding					
Birth	64	63	49	52	63	62
1 week	54	54	40	43	53	53
2 weeks	50	51	37	40	49	50
6 weeks	39	40	28	33	38	39
4 months	25	25	18	21	24	25
6 months	21	20	15	18	21	20
9 months	12	12	8	11	11	11
Base:	*2,518*	*2,419*	*1,001*	*976*	*2,756*	*2,651*

* *The data for Scotland are weighted to give a national estimate.*

Table 2.54   Prevalence of breastfeeding by region (1980, 1985 and 1990)

Age of baby	London and South East			South West and Wales			Midlands and East Anglia			North			Scotland*		
	1980	1985	1990	1980	1985	1990	1980	1985	1990	1980	1985	1990	1980	1985	1990
	Percentage breastfeeding at each age														
Birth	76	74	74	65	68	65	63	62	59	59	56	55	50	48	50
1 week	67	67	65	60	60	57	54	53	48	51	46	44	45	41	41
2 weeks	62	63	61	55	56	55	50	49	45	47	42	41	41	38	39
6 weeks	51	47	49	44	47	45	35	35	33	35	30	29	32	29	30
4 months	33	32	31	26	34	32	23	23	20	23	18	18	21	22	20
6 months	27	26	25	22	27	28	21	11	17	18	14	15	18	17	16
9 months	15	13	14	10	15	15	11	8	10	10	9	9	9	9	9
Base:	*1,284*	*1,675*	*1,785*	*483*	*657*	*666*	*808*	*960*	*1,041*	*1,179*	*1,378*	*1,452*	*1,718*	*1,895*	*1,981*

* *The data for Scotland are weighted to give a national estimate.*

3 Influences on choice of method of feeding

3.1 Introduction

The previous surveys have shown that only a minority of women who choose to bottle feed their first child subsequently breastfeed later children. Those who successfully breastfeed the first generally continue to do so for later children, and it is only those who breastfeed the first for a short time who may change to bottle feeding for later children. The earlier surveys have consequently paid particular attention to choices made by mothers having their first child.

The first survey, in 1975, examined the influences on choice of feeding method and concluded that social and cultural factors were extremely important. While some mothers would have decided on a method of feeding the baby almost as soon as they became pregnant or even before pregnancy, many would not have decided before first coming into contact with the health professionals responsible for their care during pregnancy. Such professionals are likely to be involved in providing information and advice to assist the pregnant woman to make an informed choice. In this chapter we examine in particular mothers' accounts of their contacts with health professionals and voluntary organisations providing care and advice during pregnancy.

3.2 Choice of method of feeding

In 1990, all but 7% of women said they had decided before the birth how they would feed the baby, 34% planned to bottle feed, and 59% to breastfeed. This represents, if anything, a slight fall in the proportion of women planning to breastfeed - from 61% in 1985 and 1980 (the difference is not statistically significant). Among mothers of first babies, 65% planned to breastfeed, 26% to bottle feed and 9% were undecided before the birth, again a slight drop (although not statistically signifi-

cant) from 1985 in the proportion planning to breastfeed. The 1985 and 1988 surveys detected a powerful effect, among mothers of second or subsequent children, of previous experience of breastfeeding. As Table 3.1 shows, this effect was still clear in the 1990 survey. Among mothers who had bottle fed their previous babies, 22% planned to breastfeed. Among those who had previously breastfed for less than six weeks, 45% planned to breastfeed this time, while among mothers who had breastfed an older child for six weeks or more, 88% planned to breastfeed this child. These figures are similar to those for 1985.

As in previous surveys, the vast majority of mothers who planned to breastfeed, 96%, carried out their intentions (Table 3.2). Those who appeared to change their mind from breastfeeding to bottle feeding were more likely to have had problems during the birth, with 64% having a normal delivery, than those who breastfed as planned, 77% of whom had a normal delivery.

Tables 3.3 and 3.4 show the reasons for choosing to breastfeed and bottle feed respectively. The 1990 figures are very similar to those of 1980 and 1985. By far the most common reason

Table 3.2 Proportion of mothers who actually fed their babies in the way they had planned (1980, 1985 and 1990 Great Britain)

Planned method	1980	1985	1990	1980	1985	1990
					Bases:	
Breast	97	96	96	2,592	3,156	3,186
Bottle	94	94	93	1,348	1,726	1,852
All who had decided on method before birth	96	95	95	3,940	4,882	5,038

Table 3.1 Mother's intended method of feeding according to previous experience of breastfeeding and birth order (1980, 1985 and 1990 Great Britain)

Intended method of feeding	First births			Later births												All babies		
				No experience breastfeeding			Breastfed for:						All later births					
							Less than 6 weeks			6 weeks or more								
	1980	1985	1990	1980	1985	1990	1980	1985	1990	1980	1985	1990	1980	1985	1990	1980	1985	1990
	%	%	%	%	%	%	%	%	%	%	%	%	%	%	%	%	%	%
Breast	70	67	65	22	20	22	53	45	45	91	87	88	55	55	56	61	61	59
Bottle	22	25	26	71	74	72	40	46	48	6	10	10	39	40	41	32	33	34
Had not decided	8	7	9	7	6	5	7	9	7	3	3	3	6	5	5	7	6	7
	100	100	100	100	100	100	100	100	100	100	100	100	100	100	100	100	100	100
Base:	*1,831*	*2,347*	*2,430*	*879*	*924*	*1,148*	*679*	*704*	*541*	*835*	*1,248*	*1,244*	*2,377*	*2,875*	*2,983*	*4,224*	*5,223*	*5,413*

Table 3.3   Mother's reasons for planning to breastfeed according to birth order (1980, 1985 and 1990 Great Britain)

Mother's reasons	First births			Later births			All babies		
	1980	1985	1990	1980	1985	1990	1980	1985	1990
	%	%	%	%	%	%	%	%	%
Breastfeeding is best for the baby	87	86	88	74	70	75	80	78	82
Breastfeeding is more convenient	38	30	35	41	36	38	40	33	36
Closer bond between mother and baby	24	22	24	21	20	21	22	21	23
Breastfeeding is cheaper	22	15	18	23	16	15	22	16	17
Mother's own experience	..	..	0	29	30	29	15	15	15
Breastfeeding is natural	26	19	16	19	15	11	23	17	14
Breastfeeding is best for mother	9	6	8	8	6	8	8	6	8
Cannot overfeed by breast	3	0	0	2	0	0	2	0	1
Influenced by medical personnel	2	3	3	1	1	1	2	2	2
Influenced by friends or relatives	2	2	2	1	1	1	2	2	1
No particular reason	1	2	0	2	1	1	2	2	1
Other reasons	1	1	0	2	4	1	2	3	0
Base:	1,281	1,516	1,574	1,303	1,509	1,612	2,593	3,025	3,186

Percentages do not add up to 100 as some mothers gave more than one reason.

Table 3.4   Mother's reasons for planning to bottle feed according to birth order (1980, 1985 and 1990 Great Britain)

Mother's reasons	First births			Later births			All babies		
	1980	1985	1990	1980	1985	1990	1980	1985	1990
	%	%	%	%	%	%	%	%	%
Other people can feed baby with bottle	44	45	47	35	35	34	38	38	39
Mother's own previous experience	..	..	1	47	47	39	34	31	26
Did not like the idea of breastfeeding	28	33	28	21	18	17	23	23	21
Would be embarrassed to breastfeed	17	10	10	9	4	5	11	6	7
You can see how much the baby has had	16	8	8	8	6	5	10	6	6
Medical reasons for not breastfeeding	3	4	2	4	4	4	4	4	3
Expecting to return to work soon	5	7	8	2	2	3	3	4	5
Persuaded by other people	3	2	3	2	1	0	2	1	1
No particular reason	11	7	4	4	3	3	6	4	3
Other reasons	6	10	6	4	5	5	5	6	6
Base:	403	525	629	940	1,047	1,223	1,348	1,572	1,852

Percentages do not add up to 100 as some mothers gave more than one reason.

why mothers chose to breastfeed, mentioned by 82% of those planning to breastfeed, was because they thought it best for the baby. The next most common reason, given by 36%, was that mothers felt it was more convenient. Almost a quarter of mothers planning to breastfeed felt that it helped forge a closer bond between mother and baby. Other reasons given by substantial minorities are that it is cheaper than bottle feeding (17%), and that it is natural (14%). Among mothers of second or later births, their own previous experience of breastfeeding was mentioned by 29% as motivating them to choose breastfeeding again.

The most common reason given for choosing to bottle feed was that other people can feed the baby (39%), although mothers of second and later babies most commonly cited their own experience (39%). As in 1985, mothers of first babies who chose to bottle feed were particularly likely to say that they did not like the idea of breastfeeding.

Table 3.5   Mother's intended method of feeding by how most of her friends fed their babies (1990 Great Britain)

Intended method of feeding	How mother's friends fed their babies				All mothers
	Most breastfed	Half breast/ half bottle	Most bottle fed	Don't know	
	%	%	%	%	%
Breast	84	65	46	55	59
Bottle	11	27	48	32	34
Undecided	5	8	6	13	7
	100	100	100	100	100
Base:	1,016	1,246	2,516	185	5,413 *

* Includes some cases where mother has no friends with babies.

3.3 Influence of mothers and friends on choice of method of feeding

As mentioned earlier, social and cultural factors have previously been shown to be an important influence on a woman's choice of feeding method. As Table 3.5 shows, the way a woman's friends and acquaintances feed their babies is strongly associated with her own choice. Of mothers who reported that most of their friends breastfed their babies, 84% planned to breastfeed their babies, while among mothers who said that most of their friends bottle fed, only 46% planned to breastfeed themselves. Of those whose friends were evenly divided between breast and bottle feeding 65% planned to breastfeed.

The way women were themselves fed was also strongly associated with their planned method of feeding. Table 3.6 shows that 75% of mothers who were themselves breastfed planned to breastfeed their babies, compared with 70% who were fed by both bottle and breast and 48% of those who were entirely bottle fed. Among those who did not know how they had been fed, 49% planned to breastfeed. This suggests that it may be discussions with their own breastfeeding mothers about the way they were fed which influences women to choose to breastfeed.

3.4 Contact with health professionals during the antenatal period

3.4.1 Antenatal checkups

Almost all mothers, 99%, had received antenatal care during their pregnancy. Most of these, 87%, reported that they were asked about their plans for feeding the baby during antenatal visits (Table 3.7). Significantly, however, 12% had not been asked, a figure similar to that of 1985. Mothers having their first baby were no more likely to have been asked than those having second or later children.

Since being asked about their plans for feeding could mean no more than ticking a box on a form at the booking visit, we also asked whether, during antenatal visits, there had been any discussion about methods of feeding the baby. Forty-five per cent said there had been some discussion, an increase on the 41% who had discussed feeding at antenatal visits in 1985. Mothers having their first baby were more likely to have discussed feeding (52%) than those having later children (40%).

As Table 3.8 shows (see page 36), mothers who were not asked about their plans were a little less likely to plan to breastfeed than those who were asked. However, as in 1985, having had some discussion about feeding does not appear to be related to the mothers planned method of feeding, neither for first births nor for subsequent ones.

3.4.2 Antenatal classes

Altogether, only 40% of mothers attended antenatal classes, lower than the 44% who attended in 1985. Among mothers having their first child, the figure was 67%, also lower than in 1985 when 71% of mothers having their first baby attended classes. Among mothers having second or subsequent births, 17% attended classes, compared with 22% in 1985.

Since relatively few mothers of second and subsequent babies had attended classes, analysis has been restricted to mothers of first babies.

Table 3.6 Mother's intended method of feeding by how mother was fed (1990 Great Britain)

Intended method of feeding	How mother was fed				All mothers
	Breastfed entirely	Breastfed and bottle fed	Bottle fed entirely	Don't know	
	%	%	%	%	%
Breast	75	70	47	49	59
Bottle	19	25	46	41	34
Undecided	6	5	7	10	7
	100	100	100	100	100
Base:	1,287	1,143	2,321	613	5,413

Table 3.7 Whether mothers were asked about their plans or had discussions about feeding during visits for antenatal check-ups according to birth order (1980, 1985 and 1990 Great Britain)

	First births			Later births			All babies		
	1980	1985	1990	1980	1985	1990	1980	1985	1990
	%	%	%	%	%	%	%	%	%
Not asked about plans, no discussion	12	10	12	17	11	12	15	11	12
Asked about plans, no discussion	42	41	36	47	53	47	45	47	42
Not asked about plans, had discussion	1	0	1	1	1	0	1	1	0
Asked about plans, had discussion	45	49	52	35	35	40	39	41	45
	100	100	100	100	100	100	100	100	100
Base:	1,823	2,347	2,412	2,368	2,875	2,961	4,206	5,223	5,372

Table 3.8 Proportion of mothers who planned to breastfeed by whether they had been asked their plans or discussed feeding the baby according to birth order (1980, 1985 and 1990 Great Britain)

	First births			Later births			All babies		
	1980	1985	1990	1980	1985	1990	1980	1985	1990
	Percentage planning to breastfeed								
Not asked about plans, no discussion	60	60	58	44	45	50	50	52	54
Asked about plans, no discussion	71	70	68	57	57	56	63	62	61
Had discussion*	71	67	65	57	55	54	64	62	60
Total	70	67	65	55	55	54	61	60	59
Base:									
Not asked about plans, no discussion	*223*	*239*	*283*	*395*	*314*	*360*	*618*	*553*	*643*
Asked about plans, no discussion	*754*	*929*	*849*	*1,093*	*1,484*	*1,375*	*1,847*	*2,413*	*2,224*
*Had discussion**	*855*	*1,128*	*1,248*	*887*	*1,010*	*1,169*	*1,757*	*2,138*	*2,417*
Total	*1,831*	*2,347*	*2,380*	*2,377*	*2,875*	*2,904*	*4,224*	*5,223*	*5,284*

* *Numbers to small to show those who were not asked their plans separately.*

Table 3.9 Proportion of mothers of first babies who attended antenatal classes by social class as defined by current or last occupation of husband/partner (1980, 1985 and 1990 Great Britain)

Social class	First births			*Bases:*		
	1980	1985	1990	*1980*	*1985*	*1990*
	Percentage attending antenatal classes					
I	90	92	92	*138*	*136*	*191*
II	84	84	86	*311*	*444*	*447*
IIINM	83	86	80	*179*	*213*	*201*
IIIM	65	74	69	*742*	*703*	*684*
IV	⌐56	⌐63⌐ 63	⌐60⌐ 59	⌐266	*283*	*307*
V	└	└64	└53	└	*103*	*39*
Unclassified	⌐33	⌐59⌐ 48	⌐60⌐ 41	⌐195	*81*	*126*
No partner	└	└43	└36	└	*383*	*438*
All first births	67	71	67	*1,831*	*2,347*	*2,430*

Table 3.10 Proportion of mothers of first babies who attended antenatal classes receiving certain types of advice (1980, 1985 and 1990 Great Britain)

Types of advice	1980	1985	1990
	Percentage receiving advice		
Receiving talks or discussion about feeding babies	87	86	87
Were told about advantages of breastfeeding	84	83	99
Were taught how to make up a bottle	63	59	61
Base: Mothers of first babies who attended antenatal classes	*1,228*	*1,657*	*1,624*

As in 1980 and 1985, attendance at antenatal classes was strongly associated with social class, attendance generally falling with lower social class (Table 3.9). Ninety-two per cent of mothers of first babies in Social Class I had attended classes, compared with 53% in Social Class V, and only 36% of mothers with no husband or partner. Most first time mothers had attended classes at a local clinic (57%) or a hospital (41%).

However, not all antenatal classes cover infant feeding; some deal exclusively with relaxation and preparation for the birth. But, as in previous surveys, 87% of mothers of first babies who had attended classes said that talk or discussion about infant feeding had been included (Table 3.10). Of these, the overwhelming majority (99%) said they had been told about the advantages of breastfeeding, a significant increase on the 83% of 1985. Sixty-one per cent had been taught how to make up a bottle, a similar proportion to 1985.

As in the previous two surveys, attendance at antenatal classes was associated with a higher likelihood of intending to breastfeed among women having their first child: 76% of those attending classes planned to breastfeed, compared with 43% of mothers who did not attend classes. Since attendance at classes and intentions to breastfeed are associated with social class, we have analyzed the relationship between intentions to breastfeed and attendance at antenatal classes separately for manual and non-manual social classes (Table 3.11). The table shows clearly, as in 1985, that for both manual and non-manual social classes mothers who attended classes were more likely than those who did not to plan to breastfeed.

Table 3.11 Proportion of mothers of first babies intending to breastfeed by social class as defined by current or last occupation of husband/partner and whether attended antenatal classes (1985 and 1990 Great Britain)

Social class	Attended class		Did not attend class		Total	
	1985	1990	1985	1990	1985	1990
Percentage attending antenatal classes						
Non-manual	88	81	76	62	86	78
Manual	71	74	50	43	65	63
Unclassified	66	69	42	41	56	58
No partner	51	62	29	36	38	45
All first births	76	76	47	43	67	65
Bases:						
Non-manual	684	720	108	117	793	837
Manual	760	669	327	351	1,088	1,020
Unclassified	47	74	33	50	80	124
No partner	163	155	218	278	382	433
All first births	1,655	1,618	687	796	2,343	2,414

Differences were once again, as in 1985, greater among the manual social classes than among the non-manual. Among mothers of first babies in Social Classes I, II and III non-manual, 81% of those attending classes intended to breastfeed compared with 62% of those not attending classes. Among those in Social Classes III manual, IV and V, 74% of those who went to antenatal classes planned to breastfeed, compared with 43% of those not attending classes. Substantial differences can also be seen among those whose social class was unclassified, with 69% of attenders planning to breastfeed compared with 41% of non-attenders, and women without husbands or partners, of whom 62% of attenders and 36% of non-attenders planned to breastfeed.

These results, however, cannot be interpreted to mean that going to antenatal classes has influenced women towards breastfeeding. It is also possible that women intending to breastfeed are more inclined to attend antenatal classes than are those intending to bottle feed. We do not know what the women's plans were before they attended antenatal classes. Nevertheless, as in 1985, women from manual social classes and those without husbands or partners and who could not be classified are least likely both to attend antenatal classes and to plan to breastfeed.

3.4.3 Home visits during the antenatal period

Whether or not women receive a home visit from a midwife before the birth may depend on a number of factors, including the policy and resources available in the area. Women planning to have a home delivery or to stay in hospital for a very short period after the birth are likely to receive home visits, as are mothers who are ill or otherwise unable to attend for antenatal visits. In some areas home visits are made by health visitors in order to establish contact with the expectant mothers and help build up a relationship.

All mothers were asked whether a midwife or health visitor had visited them at home in connection with their pregnancy. Overall, 54% reported having received such a visit, a similar figure to that of 1985 (Table 3.12). There was no difference between the proportion of mothers expecting their first child and those expecting their second or later child who received a visit. Visits by midwives were as common as in 1985, while visits by health visitors were slightly lower than in 1985.

Since the most common reason for home antenatal visits is in connection with early discharge from hospital, the proportion of women receiving home visits is likely to be influenced by

Table 3.12 Proportion of mothers receiving antenatal home visits by midwives and health visitors according to birth order (1980, 1985 and 1990 Great Britain)

Visit made by:	First births			Later births			All babies		
	1980	1985	1990	1980	1985	1990	1980	1985	1990
Proportion receiving antenatal home visits									
Midwife	35	44	46	50	51	49	43	48	48
Health visitor	19	15	12	22	17	13	21	16	13
Either	44	52	53	59	59	55	53	56	54
Base:	1,831	2,377	2,430	2,347	2,875	2,983	4,224	5,223	5,413

birth, rising to 35% of those giving up on days three and four, and 33% of those stopping on days five and six. Twenty-seven per cent who gave up on days one and two said they did so because the baby rejected the breast, making this the second most important reason for giving up breastfeeding in the first two days after birth. Thereafter it declines in importance, with 20% of those giving up in week two mentioning it as a reason, and 13% in week three. Among mothers giving up in the first two days after the birth, 13% had not liked breastfeeding. By the end of the first week after the birth very few gave this as a reason for stopping.

Among mothers giving up at later stages, the length of time it takes to breastfeed took on more significance as a reason for stopping. After the baby reached two months old, mothers were increasingly likely to stop breastfeeding because of returning to work. This was significantly more likely to be given as a reason in 1990 than it had been in previous surveys, but then substantially more mothers were on paid maternity leave in 1990 than in previous years. Only those who had breastfed for four months or more were most likely to say that they stopped because they had breastfed for as long as they had intended to.

As in the 1980 and 1985 surveys, women who stop breastfeeding in the early days after the birth tend to do so because they experience a variety of difficulties like painful breasts or the baby rejecting the breast. It appears either that these types of problems resolve quickly or else mothers give up the attempt to breastfeed, as they do not figure prominently as reasons for giving up at later stages.

There have been several recent initiatives to improve the support given to mothers who choose to breastfeed. The Royal College of Midwives publication *Successful Breast Feeding* was published in 1988. At the same time the Government-backed Joint Breast Feeding Initiative was launched to find new ways of helping mothers by closer collaboration between health care professionals and lay councillors from the voluntary breast feeding support group. Although 1990 was too early to expect any significant response in national statistics, the findings that the three commonest problems as perceived by mothers, namely insufficient milk, painful breasts and breast feeding taking too long, had all decreased since 1985 may reflect improved care for breastfeeding mothers. Alternatively, the finding reported in section 5.3, that since 1980, at six weeks of age breastfed babies have been increasingly likely also to receive bottle feeds, may lie at the root of the fall in the proportion reporting insufficient milk. Mothers may be moving towards more mixed breast/bottle feeding schemes for their babies at six weeks.

4.3 Breastfeeding in hospital

As in 1985, virtually all babies (100%) were delivered in hospital. The period during and immediately following the birth can affect whether breastfeeding gets off to a good start or not. Table 4.2 shows that since 1980 there has been a

Table 4.2   Length of time breastfeeding mothers stayed in hospital by birth order (1980, 1985 and 1990 Great Britain)

Length of stay	First births			Later births			All babies		
	1980	1985	1990	1980	1985	1990	1980	1985	1990
	%	%	%	%	%	%	%	%	%
2 days or less	4	7	14	41	53	62	22	30	38
3-5 days	22	44	60	29	29	26	26	36	43
6 or 7 days	41	32	19	17	10	8	29	21	14
8-10 days	28	14	5	10	6	3	19	10	4
More than 10 days	5	3	2	3	2	1	4	2	1
	100	100	100	100	100	100	100	100	100
Base:	*1,346*	*1,627*	*1,670*	*1,349*	*1,654*	*1,724*	*2,703*	*3,281*	*3,392*

* *Does not include home births.*

Table 4.3   Proportion of mothers who stopped breastfeeding before leaving hospital by birth order (1980, 1985 and 1990 Great Britain)

Length of stay	First births			Later births			All babies		
	1980	1985	1990	1980	1985	1990	1980	1985	1990
	%	%	%	%	%	%	%	%	%
Breastfeeding:	81	81	88	88	89	88	85	85	88
Breastfeeding completely	72	70	72	76	77	77	74	73	74
Breast and bottle feeding	9	11	16	12	12	11	11	12	14
Stopped breastfeeding in hospital	19	19	12	12	11	12	15	15	12
	100	100	100	100	100	100	100	100	100
Base:	*1,346*	*1,627*	*1,670*	*1,349*	*1,654*	*1,724*	*2,703*	*3,281*	*3,392*

* *Does not include home births.*

40

whose babies did not have specia
give up breastfeeding than those v

Although mothers whose babies re
more likely than those whose babi
breastfeeding by two weeks after
that by the time the baby was fou
who had received special care were
compared with 31% of those who
care. By the time the baby was six
was even more marked, with 45% o
special care no longer being breast
those who had not received specia

**Table 4.9 Proportion of mothers who h
different stages by whether o
received (1990 Great Britain**

Stage at which breastfeeding stopped	Special care received
	Percent
2 weeks	21
4 weeks	35
6 weeks	45
All breastfed babies	*405*

* *Includes some cases where it was not kno
was received.*

4.7 Birthweight

Babies may receive special care f
particularly low birthweight and pr
birthweight babies, those under 250
to breastfeed in the first place, only
once compared with 63% of thos
weight. It is therefore not surprisi
have found an association between
breastfeeding within two weeks. Ta
still the case in 1990, and there ha
1980.

**Table 4.10 Proportion of mothers who l
within two weeks by baby's
(1980, 1985 and 1990 Great**

Birthweight	1980	1985	1
	Percentage stopp breastfeeding wii two weeks		
Less than 2500g	27	24	2
2500g-2999g	22	20	2
3000g-3499g	18	19	1
3500g or more	18	18	2
All breastfed babies*	19	19	2

* *Includes some cases where birthweight wo*

Table 4.11 shows the duration of br
different weights during the first six
all stages, the lower the baby's birth
the mother to stop breastfeeding. Thi

---

decreasing trend in the length of time breastfeeding mothers stay in hospital after the baby is born. By 1990, almost two fifths of mothers left hospital within 48 hours of the birth, and four fifths left within five days. This gives hospital staff only a short time to help with problems encountered with breastfeeding in the early days, particularly with mothers breastfeeding for the first time.

The steepest drop in the prevalence of breastfeeding is in the first week after the birth, so the period in hospital is particularly important. One indication of how successful hospital policies are in helping to establish breastfeeding is the extent to which mothers who started breastfeeding are still doing so on discharge from hospital. Table 4.3 shows that 12% of women who started breastfeeding had given up before they left hospital. In 1980 and 1985, 15% had stopped by the time they left hospital, a rate which was even higher for first births. However, it is likely that the lower figure in 1990 is accounted for by the relatively shorter stay in hospital. Neither do the results suggest that women who manage to breastfeed in hospital give up when they get home where less help is available. Since altogether 20% had given up in the first two weeks, 8% gave up in the remainder of the first two weeks following discharge. In 1985, the corresponding figure was 4%, but women were at home for a greater proportion of the first two weeks after the baby's birth in 1990.

4.4 Events during labour and delivery

All previous surveys have shown that events occurring during labour and delivery can affect the initiation of breastfeeding. When complications affect her or her baby a mother who initially planned to breastfeed may change her mind. In fact, almost all of the women who did not carry out their intention to breastfeed had had some problems around the time of the birth, such as a caesarian delivery or a low birth weight baby. Nevertheless, although many mothers with these sorts of experiences did start breastfeeding, as we found previously, they were more likely than other mothers to stop breastfeeding in the first few weeks. Because the vast majority of mothers who had planned to breastfeed did, in fact, do so initially, the next few sections will look at factors which are associated with giving up breastfeeding in the first two weeks.

Although we asked questions about all types of analgesia received during labour, little effect of these on breastfeeding was found on the previous surveys. However, having a general anaesthetic was associated with stopping breastfeeding in the first two weeks. Similarly, the type of delivery most associated with breastfeeding problems was a caesarian section. In 1990, 7% of women reported having a general anaesthetic and 12% of women a caesarian delivery. This was very similar to the figures for 1985. The proportion of women having a caesarian with epidural anaesthesia, as opposed to a general anaesthetic, had increased from 33% in 1985 to 42% in 1990. The 1985 survey showed that the general anaesthetic, rather than the type of delivery, was associated with mothers giving up

---

breastfeeding during the first two weeks. This relationship still held in 1990. Altogether, 27% of women who had had a caesarian delivery stopped breastfeeding within two weeks, as did 31% of those who had a general anaesthetic. As Table 4.4 shows, women who had a caesarian delivery with epidural anaesthesia were less likely than those delivered under a general anaesthetic to stop breastfeeding within two weeks, 20% rather than 32%. In fact, mothers who had a caesarian with epidural anaesthesia were no more likely than mothers who did not have a caesarian delivery to stop breastfeeding within two weeks, 20% compared with 19%.

Table 4.4 Proportion of mothers who had stopped breastfeeding within two weeks by whether they had a general anaesthetic and/or caesarian delivery (1985 and 1990 Great Britain)

Type of delivery	Had general anaesthetic		Had other or no anaesthetic		All babies	
	1985	1990	1985	1990	1985	1990
	Percentage stooping breastfeeding within two weeks					
Caesarian	27	32	20	20	25	27
Other delivery	(1)	(1)	19	19	19	19
All babies	27	31	19	19	19	20
Bases:						
Caesarian	215	216	106	159	321	375
Other delivery	15	12	2,872	2,887	2,887	2,899
All babies	230	228	2,978	3,046	3,319*	3,395*

* *Includes some cases where type of delivery or anaesthetic was not known.*

4.5 Delays in starting breastfeeding

All previous surveys since 1975 have shown that there is a strong association between the length of time after the birth until the baby is first put to the breast and the success or failure of breastfeeding during the first two weeks. Mothers who breastfed in the first few hours were much more likely to continue than those who had started breastfeeding later.

While serious problems during the birth are likely to delay initial contact between mother and baby, and thus the start of breastfeeding, the previous surveys have shown that in the case of many mothers without such problems there has been a delay between the birth and the first attempt at breastfeeding. As Tables 4.5 and 4.6 show, there has been little change in this

Table 4.5 Length of time until mothers who breastfed first held their babies (1980, 1985 and 1990 Great Britain)

Time until mother held baby	1980	1985	1990
	%	*%*	*%*
Immediately	63	79	77
Within an hour	24	9	14
More than 1 hour, up to 12 hours later	9	9	6
More than 12 hours later	4	3	3
	100	100	100
Base:	*2,734*	*3,319*	*3,395*

Table 4.6 Length of time until bal
(1980, 1985 and 1990 Gr

Time until baby was put to the breast	19

Immediately
Within an hour
More than 1 hour, up to
4 hours later
More than 4 hours, up to
12 hours later
More than 12 hours later

1

Base: 2,7

Table 4.7 Proportion of mothers w
within two weeks by the
first put to the breast (19

Time until baby was put to the breast	1980	198
	Percentage breastfeedi two weeks	
Immediately	13	14
Within an hour	13	15
More than 1 hour, up to 4 hours later	18	21
More than 4 hours, up to 12 hours later	21	24
More than 12 hours later	32	31
Total*	19	19

* Includes some cases where the time t known.

since the 1985 survey. In 1990,
quently breastfed had held the
birth, but as Table 4.6 shows, on
breast immediately, despite so n
nity to do so. Even an hour after tl
baby to the breast. This is a slight

Table 4.8 Proportion of mothers wh
whether or not special car

Time until baby was put to the breast

Within 12 hours
More than 12 hours, up to 24 hours
More than 24 hours

All babies*

Bases:

Within 12 hours
More than 12 hours, up to 24 hours
More than 24 hours

All babies*

* Includes some cases where time until

42

5 Infant formula and bottle feeding

5.1 Introduction

In 1990, 37% of mothers gave infant formula feeds from birth. Of those who started breastfeeding 38% had stopped by six weeks and some of those who continued were giving formula as well as breastfeeds. Thus by the time they were four weeks old the majority of babies in Great Britain were being fed infant formulas and at four months three quarters of babies were fully bottle fed. It is clearly important that mothers should know how to prepare and give infant formula feeds as well as knowing how to breastfeed.

This chapter first defines the various types of infant formulas and then goes on to look at both the use of infant formula and of liquid cow's milk together with some of the problems experienced by mothers who were bottle feeding.

5.2 Definition of infant formula

Infant formulas are artificial feeds which are manufactured to take the place of human milk in providing a sole source of nutrition for the young infant. Most brands of infant formula can be classified into one of two types; either whey dominant or casein dominant, depending on whether whey or casein is the dominant protein. Whey dominant infant formulas have a whey:casein ratio which is closer to that in human milk whereas casein dominant formulas have a whey:casein ratio which is closer to that in cow's milk. Some manufacturers claim that a baby may be more satisfied by a casein dominant formula than by a whey dominant one, although there is no firm evidence to show that one type of infant formula is more suitable than the other. However, when a mother is choosing which type to give her baby she may well be influenced by such claims from manufacturers.

The majority of infant formulas which are at present available in Great Britain are based on cow's milk. Other infant formulas which are at present available in Great Britain are based on soya protein isolate as a protein source.

Follow-on milks are artificial foods intended to provide the milk drink element in the more diversified diets of older infants.

5.3 Additional bottles of milk

Mothers who breastfeed may, in addition, give their babies bottles of infant formula. For those who were still breastfeeding at the time of completing the first questionnaire, when the babies were about six weeks old, Table 5.1 shows whether bottles were also being given. The same table also shows the position at four months. Mothers were not asked details about when they gave bottles so we do not know whether they were giving them with breast milk at the same feed, or at a different feed. The second row in Table 5.1 shows that in 1990, 39% of the babies who were breastfed at six weeks were also receiving bottles. The corresponding proportions for 1985 was 34% and for 1980, 28%. Thus when the babies were about six weeks old, breastfed babies were more likely to be receiving bottles in addition to breast milk in 1990 than in 1985 or 1980. However, similar proportions of breastfed babies in 1990 and 1985 were receiving bottles when they were between four and five months old (27% in 1990 compared with 24% in 1985).

Table 5.1 Bottles given to breastfed babies at about six weeks and four months (1980, 1985 and 1990 Great Britain)

Whether bottles given	Age of baby					
	About six weeks			About four months		
	1980	1985	1990	1980	1985	1990
	%	%	%	%	%	%
No bottle given	72	66	61	81	76	73
Bottles given	28	34	39	19	24	27
	100	100	100	100	100	100
Base: breastfed babies	*1,520*	*1,720*	*1,764*	*1,021**	*1,192**	*1,182**

* Bases are the reweighted numbers.

Thus although Chapter 2 shows that there was little change in either the incidence or the duration of breastfeeding between 1985 and 1990, it appears that bottle feeding was more widespread when the babies were about six weeks old in 1990 than in 1985 as more breastfed babies were also being given bottle feeds at this stage.

5.4 The use of non-human milk at different ages

Information was collected at all three stages about the type of non-human milk being given to babies. Table 5.2 shows the results for each stage for mothers who were bottle feeding at that stage and Table 5.3 shows the results separately for mothers who were bottle feeding exclusively and for mothers who were also breastfeeding.

5.4.1 The use of infant formulas at different ages

Figure 5.1 and the second and fourth columns of Table 5.2 show that the most common type of non-human milk given

48

Figure 5.1 Main type of non-human milk given at each stage by mothers who were bottle feeding (1990 Great Britain)

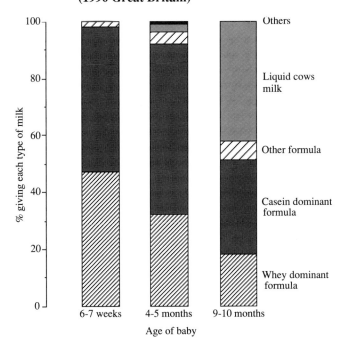

Table 5.2 Main type of non-human milk given at each stage by mothers who were bottle feeding (1985 and 1990 Great Britain)

Type of non-human milk	Mothers bottle feeding at:					
	Stage 1 (6-7 weeks)		Stage 2 (4-5 months)		Stage 3 (9-10 months)	
	1985	1990	1985	1990	1985	1990
	%	%	%	%	%	%
Whey dominant	50	47	43	32	12	18
Casein dominant	43	51	46	61	16	33
Other formula eg soya based, follow-on milk	6	2	4	4	4	7
Liquid cow's milk	0	0	7	3	67	42
Whole	0	0	6	3	60	39
Semi-skimmed	-	-	1	0	5	3
Skimmed	-	0	0	0	2	0
Other/inadequately described	-	0	1	1	1	0
	100	100	100	100	100	100
Base:	*4,072*	*4,332*	*4,313**	*4,526**	*5,048**	*5,200**

* Bases are the reweighted numbers.

when the babies were about six weeks old and when they were between four and five months old was a casein dominant infant formula, the second most common type of non-human milk was a whey dominant infant formula. Table 5.2 also shows that there is a clear trend away from using whey dominant infant formulas as the baby gets older. When the babies were about six weeks old 47% of mothers giving any non-human milk were giving a whey dominant infant formula, whereas when the babies were between four and five months old only 32% were doing so. The use of casein dominant infant formulas increased from 51% at the six weeks stage to 61% at the four to five months stage, but decreased to 33% at the nine to ten months stage as mothers were increasingly using liquid cow's milk.

Between 2% to 3% of mothers were giving a soya based formula at each stage, one mother was giving a follow-on milk at the six weeks stage, less than 1% were doing so at the four to five months stage, and 4% were giving a follow-on milk at the nine to ten months stage. Of the mothers who had given a follow-on milk, 15% had done so before the baby was four months old; the majority (68%) did not do so before the baby was six months old.

Table 5.2 also shows that there had been changes between 1985 and 1990 in the proportion of mothers using the various types of non-human milk. Casein dominant infant formulas have assumed a more prominent role since 1985. The first two columns of Table 5.2 shows that when their baby was about six weeks old more mothers were using a casein dominant infant formula in 1990 than in 1985 (51% compared with 43%), while the proportions of mothers using a whey dominant formula or another infant formula have decreased (50% in

1985 were using a whey dominant formula compared with 47% in 1990, while 6% in 1985 were using another infant formula compared with 2% in 1990).

The third and fourth columns of Table 5.2 reveals that when the babies were between four and five months old, again a higher proportion of mothers in 1990 were using a casein dominant formula compared with 1985 (61% as opposed to 46% in 1985). This increase matched a drop in the use of whey dominant formulas and liquid cow's milk. The proportion using a whey dominant formula fell from 43% in 1985 to 32% in 1990 and the proportion using liquid cow's milk decreased from 7% in 1985 to 3% in 1990. The proportion using another infant formula at the four to five months stage has remained unchanged between 1985 and 1990.

When the babies were between nine to ten months old a larger proportion of mothers were giving an infant formula in 1990 than in 1985 (57% compared with 32%) while a smaller proportion of mothers (42% compared with 67% in 1985) were giving their baby liquid cow's milk (Table 5.2).

Figure 5.2 and Table 5.3 compare the use of non-human milk by mothers bottle feeding exclusively at each stage with that by mothers who were also breastfeeding. It is noticeable that when their baby was about six weeks old and when their baby was between four to five months old, mothers who were simultaneously breast and bottle feeding were very much more likely to be giving a whey dominant than a casein dominant infant formula. The second and eighth columns of Table 5.3 show that when the babies were about six weeks old, 42% of the mothers who were exclusively bottle feeding were giving a whey dominant formula, while 73% of the mothers who were both breast and bottle feeding were using a whey dominant formula. The corresponding figures for casein dominant formulas were 56% for exclusive bottle feeders and 23%

Table 5.3 Main type of non-human milk given at each stage by mothers who were bottle feeding exclusively and mothers who were also breastfeeding (1985 and 1990 Great Britain)

Type of non-human milk	Mothers bottle feeding exclusively at:						Mothers who were also breastfeeding at:					
	Stage 1 (6-7 weeks)		Stage 2 (4-5 months)		Stage 3 (9-10 months)		Stage 1 (6-7 weeks)		Stage 2 (4-5 months)		Stage 3 (9-10 months)	
	1985	1990	1985	1990	1985	1990	1985	1990	1985	1990	1985	1990
	%	%	%	%	%	%	%	%	%	%	%	%
Whey dominant	47	42	42	30	13	18	70	73	58	62	7	15
Casein dominant	46	56	47	63	16	34	23	23	20	29	5	8
Other formula eg soya based, follow-on milk	5	2	4	3	3	7	6	3	8	6	6	10
Liquid cow's milk	0	0	5	3	67	41	0	0	12	3	78	68
Whole	0	0	5	3	59	38	0	0	11	2	67	63
Semi-skimmed	-	-	0	0	5	3	-	-	2	1	8	4
Skimmed	-	-	0	0	2	0	-	-	0	-	3	1
Other/inadequately described	-	0	1	1	1	0	-	1	3	1	4	-
	100	100	100	100	100	100	100	100	100	100	100	100
Base:	*3,503*	*3,649*	*4,031**	*4,200**	*4,758**	*4,867**	*569*	*683*	*282**	*326**	*290**	*333**

* Bases are the reweighted numbers.

Figure 5.2 Comparison of the main type of non-human milk given at each stage between mothers who were bottle feeding exclusively and those who were also breastfeeding (1990 Great Britain)

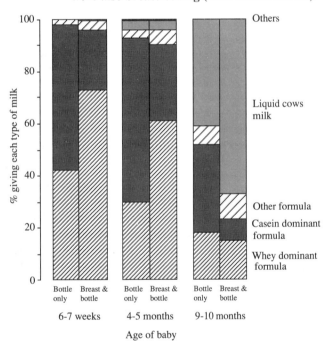

sively bottle feeding. The sixth and twelfth columns of Table 5.3 reveal that 68% of these mothers were giving liquid cow's milk, while 41% of the exclusive bottle feeders were doing so.

It was mentioned earlier that a larger proportion of mothers were giving casein dominant infant formulas in 1990 than in 1985. Table 5.3 shows that this shift to casein dominant formulas is also evident among mothers who were bottle feeding exclusively. However, the shift to casein dominant formulas since 1985 is not evident among mothers who were simultaneously breast and bottle feeding except when the babies were between four and five months old. This difference between exclusive bottle feeders and mothers who were giving both breast milk and formula may be due to the fact that mothers who simultaneously breast and bottle fed were more likely to use a whey dominant infant formula. The decrease in the proportion of mothers giving liquid cow's milk at the four to five months and nine to ten months stages is evident among both exclusive bottle feeders and those who breast and bottle fed simultaneously.

for mothers who simultaneously breast and bottle fed. Similarly, the fourth and tenth columns of Table 5.3 show that when the babies were between four and five months old, 30% of the mothers who were exclusively bottle feeding were giving a whey dominant formula while 62% of the mothers who were both breast and bottle feeding were using a whey dominant formula. The corresponding figures for casein dominant formulas were 63% for exclusive bottle feeders and 29% for mothers who simultaneously breast and bottle fed. When their baby was between nine and ten months old mothers who were simultaneously breast and bottle feeding were also more likely to be giving liquid cow's milk than those who were exclu-

Table 5.4 The use of whey and casein dominant infant formulas at different stages by those who bottle fed from birth (1985 and 1990 Great Britain)

	1985			1990		
	Stage 1 (6-7 weeks)	Stage 2 (4-5 months)	Stage 3 (9-10 months)	Stage 1 (6-7 weeks)	Stage 2 (4-5 months)	Stage 3 (9-10 months)
	%	%	%	%	%	%
Whey dominant	51	41	15	39	25	15
Casein dominant	48	49	20	59	68	39
Other	1	10	65	2	8	46
	100	100	100	100	100	100
Base:	*1,219*	*1,219**	*1,219**	*2,018*	*2,018**	*2,018**

* Bases are the reweighted numbers.

In order to get a better idea of the pattern of milk usage among bottle feeding mothers in the early weeks, Table 5.4 shows the use of whey and casein dominant formulas at different ages separately for the mothers who bottle fed from birth.

Table 5.4 shows much the same pattern as Figure 5.1 and Table 5.2, that there was a clear trend away from using whey dominant formulas as the baby got older and that the use of casein dominant formulas increased in the first ten weeks or so and then fell off as the mothers started to use other milks, mainly cow's milk.

Mothers were asked for the first time in 1990 whether they usually used a ready-to-feed infant formula which is sold ready mixed up in bottles or cartons. Table 5.5 shows that only a small proportion of mothers were using a ready-to-feed formula. The mothers were significantly more likely to be using a ready-to-feed formula at the six weeks stage; 3% of the bottle feeding mothers were using a ready-to-feed formula at this stage, compared with 2% at the four to five months stage and 1% at the nine to ten months stage.

Mothers who were simultaneously breast and bottle feeding were more likely to use a ready-to-feed formula than mothers who were exclusively bottle feeding. This was particularly so at the six weeks stage where 12% of the mothers who were both breast and bottle feeding were using a ready-to-feed formula, while only 2% of the exclusive bottle feeders were giving a ready-to-feed formula (Table 5.5). The corresponding figures for the four to five months stage were 5% for mothers who simultaneously breast and bottle fed and 1% for exclusive bottle feeders.

Table 5.5 The use of ready-to-feed infant formulas at different stages (1990 Great Britain)

Stage	Mothers bottle feeding exclusively at the stage	Mothers who were also breastfeeding at the stage	All bottle feeding mothers at the stage
	Percentage using a ready-to-feed formula		
Stage 1 (6-7 weeks)	2	12	3
Stage 2 (4-5 months)	1	5	2
Stage 3 (9-10 months)	1	1	1
Bases:			
Stage 1 (6-7 weeks)	*3,649*	*683*	*4,332*
Stage 2 (4-5 months)	*4,200*	*326*	*4,526*
Stage 3 (9-10 months)	*4,867*	*333*	*5,200*

5.4.2   Choice of type of infant formula

It seems from the above analyses that mothers who bottle feed move from using whey dominant formulas as the baby gets older. This section looks at the changes made by individual mothers in the type of formula they used. On the first stage questionnaire mothers were asked whether they had changed from using one infant formula to another, and if so why they had stopped using the first one. Of the mothers who were bottle feeding at six to ten weeks, 41% had changed the type of infant formula they were giving; a fall from 44% in 1985.

Table 5.6 shows that the most common reason for changing the type of infant formula was because the mother thought the baby was still hungry or not satisfied. This reason was given for 79% of the changes made. In addition, 15% of the changes were due to the baby being sick and 10% of the changes were because the baby was constipated. Three per cent of the changes were made because of suspected allergy.

Compared with 1985, mothers in 1990 were more likely to change brands because they felt that the baby was hungry or not satisfied by the formula. Mothers in 1990 were less likely to change brands because the baby was sick. Table 5.6 shows that the proportion of changes due to the baby being hungry rose from 69% in 1985 to 79% in 1990, while the proportion of changes caused by the baby being sick fell from 18% in 1985 to 15% in 1990.

Table 5.6 Reasons given by mothers for changing infant formula (1985 and 1990 Great Britain)

Reason for changing infant formula	1985	1990
	Percentage giving reason	
Still hungry/not satisfied	69	79
Kept being sick	18	15
Constipation	10	10
Allergy	3	3
Other reason	10	7
Base: number of changes	*2,427*	*1,956*

Percentages do not add up to 100 as some mothers gave more than one reason for a particular change.

5.4.3   The use of liquid cow's milk

As Table 5.2 and Figure 5.1 have shown, less than 1% of mothers who were giving any non-human milk were giving their babies liquid cow's milk at the time the first questionnaire was completed. When the babies were between four and five months old, this figure had risen to 3% and by the time their baby was between nine and ten months old, 42% of bottle feeding mothers were giving liquid cow's milk. However, more mothers (58%) were giving infant formula when their baby was between nine and ten months old.

Table 5.7 Liquid cow's milk given at stage 3 (9-10 months) (1985 and 1990 Great Britain)

Proportion of mothers who gave liquid cow's milk	1985	1990
As main milk:	64	40
Whole	57	37
Semi-skimmed	5	3
Skimmed	2	0
As second milk:	15	17
Whole	11	14
Semi-skimmed	3	3
Skimmed	1	0
To mix food	78	68
All using liquid cow's milk	88	76
Base:	*5,223**	*5,413**

* Bases are the reweighted numbers.
Percentages do not add to 100 as some mothers gave liquid cow's milk in more than one way.

On the third stage questionnaire mothers were asked what type of milk they were giving as the main milk, as a second milk and to mix solid food. The second column of Table 5.7 shows that by the time the babies were between nine and ten months old, 76% of all mothers were giving their baby liquid cow's milk in some way; a fall from 88% in 1985. The most common usage of liquid cow's milk at this age was to mix food (68%), next came giving it as the main milk (40%), and relatively few mothers were giving it as the second milk (17%). It has been mentioned earlier that there has been a fall in the use of liquid cow's milk since 1985; Table 5.7 confirms this and shows that since 1985 both the proportion of mothers giving liquid cow's milk as the main drink and the proportion using it to mix food have declined.

The vast majority of mothers who were giving their babies liquid cow's milk were giving whole cow's milk. However, 7% of those giving cow's milk as the main milk and 21% of those giving it as a second milk were giving either semi-skimmed or skimmed milk; a decline from the proportion of 10% for main milk and 26% for the second milk in 1985. Despite the fall in the use of semi-skimmed and skimmed milk since 1985, the proportions using these types of liquid cow's milk still pose a concern as it is recommended in *Present day practice in infant feeding: third report*[1] that fully skimmed and semi-skimmed milks are not suitable for an infant's diet.

At stage three mothers were asked at what age they had first given the milks they were currently using, either as a drink or to mix solid food. Thus we can examine the age at which liquid cow's milk is first introduced into the young child's diet. Figure 5.3 shows the earliest age at which liquid cow's milk was given at all, one can see from this that in most cases it was not until the baby was over 6 months old that liquid cow's milk had been introduced. Table 5.8 shows the earliest age at which liquid cow's milk was given for the three types of usage: to mix solid food, as a main drink, and as a second drink. The last column of Table 5.8 shows that only 11% of mothers had given liquid cow's milk before the baby was 5 months old; this was generally to mix solid food rather than as a drink. Only 3% of mothers had given liquid cow's milk as the main drink before 5 months, and only 36% of the mothers had given liquid cow's milk as the main drink by the time their baby was nine months old.

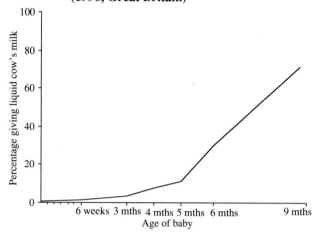

Figure 5.3 **Age by which mother had introduced liquid cow's milk into the baby's diet (1990, Great Britain)**

5.5 Help with the cost of milk for the baby

In 1990 all pregnant women and families with a child under five who were on income support were entitled to tokens for free milk or infant formula. At each stage of the survey mothers were asked whether they got milk tokens and Table 5.9 shows the results. The proportions of mothers receiving tokens was about 20% at each stage (a decrease from the 1985 figure of around 30%). Not surprisingly receiving milk tokens was strongly related to social class with those in the lower social classes or with no partner being the most likely to get milk tokens.

Table 5.9 **Whether mothers received milk tokens at different stages (1985 and 1990 Great Britain)**

Whether mother received milk tokens	Stage 1 (6-7 weeks)		Stage 2 (4-5 months)		Stage 3 (9-10 months)	
	1985	1990	1985	1990	1985	1990
	%	%	%	%	%	%
Yes	31	22	30	23	28	22
No, did not receive tokens	69	78	70	77	72	78
	100	100	100	100	100	100
Base:	5,223	5,413	5,223*	5,413*	5,223*	5,413*

* Bases are the reweighted numbers.

Table 5.8 **Age by which mothers had introduced liquid cow's milk to mix solid food, as a main drink, or as a second drink (1985 and 1990 Great Britain)**

	Proportion of mothers who gave liquid cow's milk:							
	To mix food		As main drink		As second drink		At all	
	1985	1990	1985	1990	1985	1990	1985	1990
Before 6 weeks	1	0	0	1	0	0	1	1
Before 3 months	3	1	1	1	0	0	3	3
Before 4 months	8	5	2	2	0	0	9	7
Before 5 months	14	9	4	3	1	1	16	11
Before 6 months	39	26	23	11	3	3	45	30
Before 9 months	74	63	59	36	12	13	84	71
Base:*	5,223	5,413	5,223	5,413	5,223	5,413	5,223	5,413

* Bases are re-weighted numbers.

5.6 Problems with bottle feeding in hospital

Mothers who bottle feed as well as those who breast feed can experience problems feeding their baby in the early weeks. As the majority of mothers will give their baby infant formula at some stage it is important that all mothers, regardless of how they intend to feed their baby, should know how to make up a bottle of infant formula so as to minimise possible feeding problems. In 1990, 83% of the mothers attended a talk or discussion on infant feeding at antenatal classes and 61% of these mothers were taught how to make up bottles of milk at these classes (a decrease from 69% in 1985). In addition, mothers who planned to breastfeed were less likely to have been taught how to make up a bottle at antenatal classes. Sixty-seven per cent of those intending to bottle feed, compared with 59% of those intending to breastfeed had received such tuition. (The 1985 survey found that mothers who planned to breastfeed were just as likely to have been taught how to make up a bottle as mothers who planned to bottle feed.) Despite the importance of learning how to make up a bottle, a significant minority of mothers in 1990 were not taught how to do so at antenatal classes.

Bottle feeding mothers were less likely than breastfeeding mothers to have experienced problems feeding their baby while in hospital. Even so, 17% had problems and not surprisingly mothers of first babies were more likely than other mothers to have had such problems, 19% compared with 16%. Table 5.10 shows the feeding problems that bottle feeding mothers had. The last column of the table shows that the most common problems mentioned were the baby being ill and the baby being sick; respectively 30% and 24% of the mothers experienced these problems. Mothers experienced much the same sorts of problems regardless of whether it was their first baby or not. The situation in 1985 was similar to that in 1990 except that a larger proportion of mothers in 1990 had problems because their baby disliked the milk (23% compared with 12% in 1985).

When asked whether they were able to get help and advice on feeding while they were in hospital, 85% said they were able to get help. The majority of mothers who received help or advice about feeding while they were still in hospital got help from nurses (66%). Just under half of the mothers who had help obtained it from midwives and a fifth received help from doctors.

5.7 Problems with bottle feeding at home

Of those mothers who were bottle feeding when they left hospital, 19% experienced some problems feeding their baby after they had returned home; a fall from 22% in 1985. Table 5.11 shows the problems that these mothers had. The sorts of problems experienced by bottle feeding mothers were similar regardless of birth order. By far the most common problem now that the babies were a bit older was that the baby appeared to be hungry, the last column of Table 5.11 shows that 33% of the bottle feeding mothers had this problem. Chapter 4 shows that the mother's perception that the baby was hungry was also the most common problem experienced by breastfeeders. However, compared to 1985, Table 5.11 reveals that a smaller proportion of mothers said that they had problems because the baby appeared to be hungry (33% compared with 43% in 1985). The last column of Table 5.11 reveals that besides the baby appearing to be hungry other common problems the mothers experienced included the baby being sick (22%) and the baby having wind (20%). In addition, compared with 1985, a significantly larger proportion of mothers in 1990 had problems because the baby disliked the milk (15% compared with 9% in 1985).

The vast majority of mothers who had problems with bottle feeding (90%) received some sort of professional help or advice with these problems. Mothers having their first baby were more likely to have received help or advice than mothers who were having their second or subsequent baby (94%

Table 5.10 Feeding problems as reported by bottle feeding mothers while in hospital by birth order (1985 and 1990 Great Britain)

Feeding problem	First births		Later births		All babies	
	1985	1990	1985	1990	1985	1990
	Percentage having problem					
Baby hungry	17	16	13	11	15	13
Baby ill	31	27	33	32	32	30
Baby did not like milk	12	25	12	22	12	23
Baby vomiting	23	21	26	27	25	24
Baby got too much/ too little wind	9	11	5	6	7	8
Baby could not latch on to breast	-	2	1	4	0	3
Baby constipated	0	0	2	1	1	1
Other	21	6	21	11	21	9
Base:	129	141	165	185	294	326

Percentages do not add up to 100 as some mothers experienced more than one type of feeding problem.

Table 5.11 Feeding problems as reported by bottle feeding mothers after leaving hospital by birth order (1985 and 1990 Great Britain)

Feeding problem	First births		Later births		All babies	
	1985	1990	1985	1990	1985	1990
	Percentage having problem					
Baby hungry	45	36	41	31	43	33
Baby ill	11	9	14	11	12	10
Baby did not like milk	10	16	8	15	9	15
Baby vomiting	17	20	21	24	19	22
Baby got too much/ too little wind	17	22	16	19	17	20
Baby constipated	7	4	6	7	6	6
Sore/cracked nipples	4	6	5	4	4	5
Baby could not latch on to breast	1	4	1	2	1	3
Other	10	8	14	7	12	8
Base:	278	216	336	288	614	504

Percentages do not add up to 100 as some mothers experienced more than one type of feeding problem.

compared with 88%). Now that they had left hospital, the most likely person to have advised the mothers on such matters was the health visitor; 60% of mothers said that they had been helped or advised by her. Other common sources of advice and help with bottle feeding when the mother had returned home were midwives or nurses, family doctors, and friends and relatives. Respectively 48%, 31% and 19% of the bottle feeding mothers received help from these sources. In contrast, only 8% of bottle feeding mothers received help or advice from doctors at the child health clinic.

Reference

[1] *Present day practice in infant feeding: third report.* Report on Health and Social Subjects 32. DHSS (1988).

6 Solid food, vitamins and other drinks

6.1 Introduction

Present day practice in infant feeding: third report states that very few infants will require solid food before the age of three months, but the vast majority should be offered a mixed diet not later than the age of six months. This chapter discusses the age at which mothers introduced solid food, what sorts of solid food they were giving to babies at different ages, what factors influenced them in their choice of solid food, and the use of additional drinks and vitamin supplements. It also goes on to look at some of the problems mothers faced once the baby had got a bit older.

6.2 Age of introduction of solid food

In 1990, mothers were a little less likely to have introduced solid food before eight weeks than they were in 1985. Table 6.1 and Figure 6.1 show that 19% had introduced solid food before eight weeks compared with 24% in 1985. However, mothers in 1990 were significantly more likely to have introduced solid food before their baby was three months old. In 1990, 68% of babies had been given solid food by the time they were three months old compared with 62% in 1985. As in 1980 and 1985 virtually all babies had been given solid food by the time they were six months old. *Present day practice in infant feeding: third report*[1] states that very few infants will require solid food before the age of three months; it is clear that in 1990 many mothers were still starting solid food earlier than is generally thought desirable.

Table 6.1 Proportion of babies who had been given solid food by different ages (1980, 1985 and 1990 Great Britain)

Age of baby	1980	1985	1990
	Percentage giving solid food		
4 weeks	4	3	3
6 weeks	14	11	9
8 weeks	24	24	19
3 months	56	62	68
4 months	89	90	94
6 months	98	99	99
9 months	99	100	100
Base:	*4,224*	*5,223*	*5,413*

The age at which the mother introduced solid food was examined in more detail in 1990 to find out about the rate at which solid food was introduced. The results are presented in Table 6.2. Less than 1% of the mothers introduced solid food in the first two weeks, but between the third and fifth week the rate of introduction of solid food increased slightly and between 1% and 2% more mothers introduced solid food each week. The rate grew again from the sixth to the eighth week

Figure 6.1 Proportion of babies who had been given solid food by different ages (1980, 1985 and 1990, Great Britain)

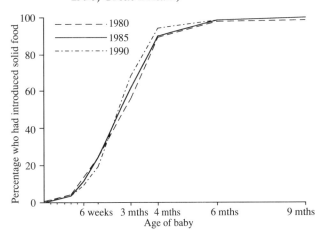

Table 6.2 Rate at which mothers introduced solid food in the first four months (1990 Great Britain)

Age of baby	Percentage of mothers who introduced solid food per week
1 week	0
2 weeks	0
3 weeks	1
4 weeks	2
5 weeks	1
6 weeks	5
7 weeks	4
8 weeks	6
Between 9 weeks to just under 12 weeks	10
Between 12 weeks and 16 weeks	6
Mothers who had not introduced solid food by 16 weeks	6
Base:	*5,413*

when between 4% and 6% more mothers began giving solid food each week. The final growth in the rate occurred between the ninth to twelfth week when each week 10% more mothers started offering solid food. The rate then slowed down between the thirteenth to sixteenth week when around 6% more mothers introduced solid food each week. Thus, contrary to the statement in *Present day practice in infant feeding: third report*[1] that few infants will require solid food before the age of three months, the rate at which mothers introduced solid food in 1990 began to grow from about the sixth week and distinctly large proportions of mothers started giving solid food between the ages of eight weeks and three months.

The range of normal weights and lengths for babies at any given age is very wide. This raise the question whether it is possible that bigger babies are physically more advanced and have a more demanding appetite which is more difficult to satisfy. The 1990 survey only collected information on

Table 6.3   Age at introduction of solid food by birthweight (1990 Great Britain)

Age at introduction of solid food	Birthweight of baby				All babies
	Less than 2500g	2500-2999g	3000-3499g	3500g or more	
	Percentage giving solid food				
4 weeks	2	2	3	3	3
6 weeks	7	6	9	10	9
8 weeks	15	16	18	22	19
3 months	59	66	67	72	68
4 months	89	92	94	96	94
6 months	98	99	99	100	99
9 months	100	100	100	100	100
Base:	295	884	1,987	2,063	5,229

* *Excludes some cases where age at introduction of solid food was not known.*

birthweight and did not have any data on the weight or length of the baby when the mother completed any of the questionnaires. However, birthweight can be used as an indicator of weight in later infancy because babies growing normally will grow at a rate related to their birthweight. Thus, although birthweight does not necessarily predict the weight of a baby at different ages it gives a satisfactory indication of the weight in later infancy.

Table 6.3 and Figure 6.2 reveal that before their baby was four months old mothers of higher birthweight babies tended to introduce solid food earlier. Birthweight however, had little effect on the introduction of solid food beyond the age of four months. Table 6.3 shows that 72% of the mothers of babies born weighing 3,500 grammes or more had introduced solid food by the time their baby was three months old compared with around 66% of mothers of babies born with lower weights. Table 6.3 also indicates that mothers of babies born weighing 3,500 grammes or more were significantly more

likely to have introduced solid food by eight weeks than mothers of babies with lower birthweight (22% compared with between 15% and 18% among mothers of lower birth weight babies). The figures above indicate that before the age of four months higher birthweight babies tended to start solid food earlier than lower birthweight babies. However, this difference may not be related to the difficulty in satisfying the hunger of higher birthweight babies. Information was collected at all three stages on whether the mothers had problems feeding their baby and the reasons for the feeding problems. An examination of the feeding problems by birthweight shows that mothers of lower birthweight babies were just as likely to have difficulties satisfying their baby's hunger as mothers of higher birthweight babies. Thus it is not possible to conclude that mothers of higher birthweight babies tended to introduce solid food earlier because they had more difficulty in satisfying their baby's hunger.

All the previous surveys found an association between the age at which solid food was started and the method of feeding: mothers who bottle fed started solid food earlier than those who breastfed. Table 6.4 shows that this was still the case in 1990, 12% of mothers who were bottle feeding had given solid food by six weeks compared with only 2% of mothers who were breastfeeding.

Previous surveys revealed that the age at introduction to solid food is strongly related to social class as defined by the current or most recent occupation of the husband/partner. Table 6.5 and Figure 6.3 show that the regular pattern of an earlier introduction of solid food in each consecutive social class group was again apparent in 1990. In 1990 mothers with no husband or partner were the most likely to have introduced solid food by three months, the minimum recommended age

Figure 6.2   Age at introduction of solid food by birthweight (1990)

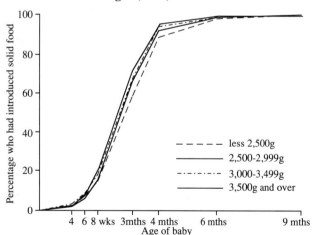

Table 6.4   Proportion of babies who had been given solid food by six weeks according to method of feeding (1980, 1985 and 1990 Great Britain)

Method of feeding at six weeks	1980	1985	1990	1980	1985	1990
	Percentage giving solid food			*Bases*:		
Breast	4	4	2	166	1,711	1,764
Bottle	21	14	12	2,487	3,483	3,649
Total	14	11	9	4,208	5,194	5,413

* *Includes some cases for whom the method of feeding at six weeks was not known.*

Table 6.5   Age at introduction of solid food by social class as defined by current or last occupation of husband/partner (1985 and 1990 Great Britain)

Age at introduction of solid food	Social class																Total	
	I		II		IIINM		IIIM		IV		V		No partner		Unclassified			
	1985	1990	1985	1990	1985	1990	1985	1990	1985	1990	1985	1990	1985	1990	1985	1990	1985	1990
	Percentage giving solid food																	
4 weeks	2	1	2	1	2	2	3	3	4	2	5	6	7	4	3	4	3	3
6 weeks	5	2	6	5	8	8	12	10	13	10	17	15	21	14	10	10	11	9
8 weeks	10	9	16	13	17	17	26	20	28	22	36	24	38	28	23	20	24	19
3 months	44	57	53	61	58	70	65	69	67	73	72	72	73	76	58	68	62	68
4 months	84	91	87	92	88	96	92	94	92	96	93	95	92	95	84	94	90	94
6 months	98	100	99	99	99	99	99	99	99	100	100	99	99	99	96	99	99	99
9 months	100	100	100	100	100	100	100	100	100	100	100	100	100	100	99	100	100	100
Base:*	*301*	*385*	*1,021*	*1,007*	*439*	*412*	*1,631*	*1,556*	*738*	*726*	*245*	*115*	*546*	*728*	*171*	*300*	*5,092*	*5,229*

* *Excludes some cases where the age at introduction of solid food was not known.*

Figure 6.3 Age at introduction of solid food by social class as defined by current or last occupation of husband/partner (1990, Great Britain)

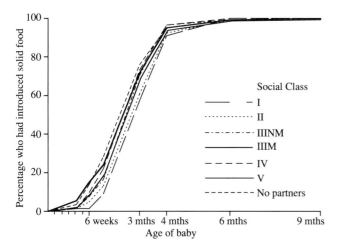

for starting solid food; 76% had given solid food by three months, compared with 57% in Social Class I. These results might be explained by the higher prevalence of bottle feeding among mothers in the lower social class groups. However, when the results were examined separately for breast and bottle feeding mothers within each social class group, the differences between the social class groups were still apparent.

The overall picture observed earlier of mothers being more likely to have introduced solid food by three months than they were in 1985 was true in every social class group, except mothers in Social Class V for whom there had been no change since 1985 (Table 6.5).

Table 6.6 and Figure 6.4 show that in 1990, as in 1985, mothers in Scotland introduced solid food earlier than their counterparts in England and Wales. Within England and Wales the further north one goes the earlier was the age at introduction to solid food. This pattern was apparent even after allowing for the fact that mothers in the north were more likely than those in the south to bottle feed.

Figure 6.4 Introduction of solid food by region (1990, Great Britain)

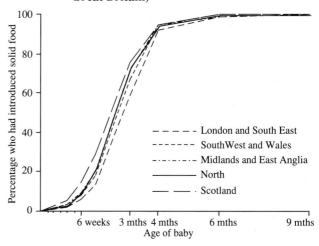

Table 6.6   Age at introduction of solid food by region (1985 and 1990 Great Britain)

Age at introduction of solid food	1990						1985					
	London & South East	South West & Wales	Midlands & East Anglia	North	Scotland	Total	London & South East	South West & Wales	Midlands & East Anglia	North	Scotland	Total
	Percentage giving solid food											
4 weeks	2	3	3	3	5	3	2	3	5	3	6	3
6 weeks	6	8	9	10	15	9	7	11	13	13	18	11
8 weeks	14	18	20	22	29	19	16	25	27	27	32	24
3 months	59	67	72	74	76	68	55	61	67	67	64	62
4 months	92	95	95	95	95	94	87	89	90	93	90	90
6 months	99	100	99	100	100	99	99	99	98	99	99	99
9 months	100	100	100	100	100	100	100	100	100	100	100	100
Base:*	*1,665*	*641*	*1,028*	*1,437*	*458*	*5,229*	*1,580*	*655*	*978*	*1,340*	*539*	*5,092*

* *Excludes some cases where the age at introduction of solid food was not known.*

Figure 6.5 Age at introduction of solid food by smoking (1990, Great Britain)

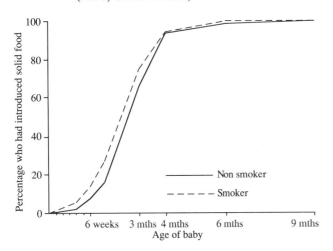

It was mentioned earlier that, compared with 1985, mothers in 1990 were a little less likely to have introduced solid food before eight weeks but were more likely to have done so before the baby was three months old. Table 6.6 reveals that this difference can be observed in all five regions.

In 1990 mothers who smoked during pregnancy were likely to have introduced solid food earlier than mothers who did not smoke (Figure 6.5). Table 6.7 shows that 75% of those who smoked during pregnancy had introduced solid food by three months, compared with 66% of those who did not smoke during pregnancy. As already demonstrated, smoking is strongly related to social class but smokers within each social class group had given solid food earlier than non-smokers. This relationship between smoking and the early introduction of solid food is also evident if one looks at the mother's smoking habits before rather than during pregnancy.

Table 6.8 presents the figures on the age at introduction to solid food by mothers who drank alcohol during pregnancy and those who abstained from alcohol in 1990. As in the analysis on breastfeeding and drinking habits the women in the sample have been divided into three groups, namely drinkers (those who drank one or more units of alcohol a week

during pregnancy), light drinkers (those who drank less than one unit of alcohol a week), and non-drinkers (those who did not drink alcohol at all during pregnancy). The final three columns of Table 6.8 show that drinking habits during pregnancy did not seem to affect the introduction of solid food before eight weeks; similar proportions of drinkers, light drinkers and non-drinkers introduced solid food at four, six and eight weeks. (But from three months onwards drinkers introduced solid food the earliest, followed by light drinkers. Non-drinkers were the latest in introducing solid food from the age of three months.)

The relationship between drinking habits and the introduction of solid food was not replicated in every social class group in 1990. Drinking habits did not seem to affect the introduction of solid food among women in Social Classes III manual and IV. None of the differences for these three groups was statistically significant. Non-drinkers in Social Class I were less likely to introduce solid food by eight weeks and four months; 4% of non-drinkers in Social Class I had introduced solid food by eight weeks compared with between 10% and 11% of drinkers and light drinkers, and 88% of non-drinkers had introduced solid food by four months compared with between 92% and 96% of drinkers and light drinkers. Light drinkers in Social Class II were more likely to introduce solid food by four months; 95% of them had introduced solid food by this time compared with 88% of drinkers and 91% of non-drinkers. Drinkers in Social Class III non-manual were less likely to introduce solid food at four and six weeks; at six weeks 3% of drinkers had introduced solid food compared with 7% of light drinkers and 11% of non-drinkers. Drinkers among women in Social Class V and those not living with a husband/partner introduced solid food earlier than light drinkers, and non-drinkers were the latest in this group to introduce solid food; at four months, 99% of drinkers had introduced solid food while 96% of light drinkers and 93% of non-drinkers had done so. Finally, drinkers among women whose social class could not be classified were more likely to have introduced solid food at six and eight weeks; at six weeks 19% of drinkers had introduced solid food compared with 11% of light drinkers and 5% of non-drinkers. However at three and four months,

Table 6.7   Age at introduction of solid food by smoking (1985 and 1990 Great Britain)

Age at introduction of solid food	Smoking status during pregnancy					
	1990			1985		
	Non-smoker	Smoker	Total	Non-smoker	Smoker	Total
	Percentage giving solid food					
4 weeks	2	5	3	2	5	3
6 weeks	7	14	9	8	17	11
8 weeks	16	27	19	19	33	24
3 months	66	75	68	58	70	62
4 months	94	95	94	88	92	90
6 months	99	100	99	99	99	99
9 months	100	100	100	100	100	100
Base*:	3,800	1,429	5,229	3,651	1,441	5,092

* Excludes some cases where the age at introduction of solid food was not known.

Table 6.8 Age at introduction of solid food by whether mother drank alcohol during pregnancy or not and by social class as defined by current or last occupation of husband/partner (1990 Great Britain)

Age at introduction of solid food	Social class											
	I			II			IIINM			IIIM		
	Non-drinker	Light drinker*	Drinker†	Non-drinker	Light drinker*	Drinker†	Non-drinker	Light drinker*	Drinker†	Non-drinker	Light drinker*	Drinker†
Percentage still breastfeeding												
4 weeks	-	1	-	2	1	1	4	1	0	4	3	4
6 weeks	2	3	3	6	5	2	11	7	3	11	9	11
8 weeks	4	10	11	11	15	10	15	16	19	22	19	22
3 months	50	59	63	58	63	59	69	70	73	68	69	72
4 months	88	92	96	91	95	88	94	95	97	96	93	94
6 months	100	99	100	99	99	99	98	100	100	99	100	98
9 months	100	100	100	100	100	100	100	100	100	100	100	100
*Base**:*	*114*	*194*	*77*	*276*	*543*	*189*	*123*	*216*	*74*	*476*	*740*	*340*

Table 6.8 - *continued*

Age at introduction of solid food	Social class									All mothers		
	IV			V and no partner			Unclassified					
	Non-drinker	Light drinker*	Drinker†	Non-drinker	Light drinker*	Drinker†	Non-drinker	Light drinker*	Drinker†	Non-drinker	Light drinker*	Drinker†
Percentage still breastfeeding												
4 weeks	2	3	3	4	2	4	2	5	3	3	2	3
6 weeks	9	10	11	11	14	14	5	11	19	9	9	9
8 weeks	22	21	23	24	28	31	14	22	28	18	19	21
3 months	71	72	78	73	76	80	62	75	64	66	69	71
4 months	94	97	95	93	96	99	88	98	94	93	95	94
6 months	100	100	99	100	100	99	97	99	100	99	100	99
9 months	100	100	100	100	100	100	100	100	100	100	100	100
*Base**:*	*266*	*313*	*147*	*271*	*347*	*222*	*118*	*130*	*52*	*1,646*	*2,487*	*1,097*

*   *Light drinkers are defined as women who drank less than one unit of alcohol a week during pregnancy.*
†   *Drinkers are defined as women who drank one unit of alcohol a week during pregnancy.*
** *Excludes some cases where the age at introduction of solid food was not known.*

light drinkers were the most likely to have introduced solid food; at three months 75% of light drinkers had introduced solid food compared with 64% of drinkers and 62% of non-drinkers.

6.3 Solid foods given at different ages

Mothers who had introduced solid food by the time the first questionnaire was completed were asked what they had given as the first solid food. Their answers are presented in Table 6.9. As in previous years cereal and rusks were by far the most common first solid food for babies under six weeks old: fifty-one percent of the mothers gave rusks as the first solid food and 44% gave cereal as the first solid food. Nearly all (95%) of the mothers who gave cereal as the first food gave rice cereal. In 1990, as in 1985, the majority of mothers who gave cereal as the first food (62%) gave unsweetened cereal while 92% of mothers who gave rusks as a first food gave sweetened rusks. At all stages mothers were asked to list all the solid food their baby had eaten on the previous day. The different foods mentioned at each stage by all the mothers who had given some solid food on the previous day are set out in Table 6.10.

In 1990, mothers who gave solid food at six weeks tended to give rusks and cereal. Table 6.10 shows that 52% of the

Table 6.9 First type of solid food given by those who had introduced solids by six weeks (1985 and 1990 Great Britain)

First type of solid food given	1980	1985	1990
	%	%	%
Rusk	56	52	51
Rice cereal	⎱35	⎱42	42 ⎱44
Other cereal			2
Dried, tinned or jars of food	4	3	4
Fresh/homemade	1	1	1
Other	4	2	0
	100	100	100
Base:	*605*	*559*	*453*

mothers had given cereal and 48% had given rusks the day before they completed the Stage 1 questionnaire. Rice cereal was the most popular cereal given. A comparison of the solid food given to the baby at the six week stage between 1990 and 1985 suggests that mothers in 1990 were more likely to give baby food and less likely to give rusks. The proportion of mothers who gave rusks fell by six percentage points between 1985 and 1990 while the proportion of mothers who gave baby food rose by six percentage points.

By about four months the majority of the babies were having solid food. Commercial baby food was the most common food

Table 6.10 Proportion of mothers who had given different kinds of food on one day at six weeks (stage 1), four months (stage 2) and at nine months (stage 3)

Type of food	6 weeks 1985	6 weeks 1990	4 months 1985	4 months 1990	9 months 1985	9 months 1990
	Percentage giving each food					
Rice cereal*	⎤ 52	37 ⎤ 52	⎤ 65	13 ⎤ 57	⎤ 84	4 ⎤ 86
Other cereal*	⎟	15 ⎦	⎟	44 ⎦	⎟	82 ⎦
Rusk	54 ⎦	48 ⎦	40 ⎦	35	28 ⎦	24
Dried babyfood†	⎤ 30	⎤ 36	⎤ 82	49 ⎤ 95	⎤ 52	20 ⎤ 62
Tinned or jarred babyfood†	⎦	⎦	⎦	46 ⎦	⎦	42 ⎦
Homemade food**	3	4	35	27		
Other food**	2	1	8	13		
Yoghurt					26	24
Fresh fruit					26	26
Other dessert					21	24
Egg					21	8
Cheese and dairy produce					9	13
Meat					37	31
Fish					9	9
Potatoes					47	42
Other vegetables					49	47
Casserole/stew					12	18
Soup					7	7
Bread					64	54
Other foods					11	14
Base: all mothers who had given solid food	1,299	1,263	4,930††	5,097††	5,138††	5,272††

*   Not known whether baby or adult cereal.   †   Commercially prepared tinned or dried food.
** Itemised in Stage 3 questionnaire only.   †† Bases are the reweighted numbers.

given at this stage; 95% of the mothers gave commercial baby food (Table 6.10). In 1990 mothers who gave commercial baby food were just as likely to give ready-mixed baby food in tins or jars as dried baby food which required mixing in liquid; 46% gave baby food in tins and jars while 49% gave dried baby food. At about four months mothers who gave cereal were less likely to give rice cereal; 13% gave rice cereal while 44% gave other cereal. As in 1985 only a minority of mothers (27%) gave home made food.

Compared with 1985, mothers in 1990 were less likely to give cereal, rusk and homemade food at the four months stage. Table 6.10 shows that 57% of mothers in 1990 gave cereal compared with 65% in 1985, 35% gave rusks in 1990 as opposed to 40% in 1985, and 27% gave homemade food in 1990 while 35% did so in 1985. In contrast, a larger proportion of mothers in 1990 than in 1985 gave commercial baby food (95% compared with 82%).

By the time the babies were around nine months old they were given a range of food. Babies who were given commercial baby food were more likely to be given ready made up food in tins and jars than to be given dried baby food; 42% were given baby food in tins or jars while 20% were given dried baby food.

The types of food given to babies aged nine months in 1990 differed slightly from the ones given in 1985. As Table 6.10 shows a smaller proportion of babies were given rusks in 1990 (24% compared with 28% in 1985). Among the homemade food given to the baby the most significant change was a large fall in the proportion given eggs (8% were given eggs in 1990 compared with 21% in 1985). The reason for this fall was not collected in the questionnaire but the decrease could be due to concern about the risk of salmonella infection in eggs. In addition mothers seemed to have switched from yoghurt to other desserts between 1985 and 1990. The proportion of mothers giving yoghurt fell by two percentage points while the proportion of mothers giving other desserts rose by three percentage points. There has also been a slight fall in the proportion of mothers giving potatoes, vegetables, bread and meat. However, the fall in the proportion giving meat, potatoes and vegetables may not be a real decline because the proportion giving casserole and stew, which often contain meat, potatoes and vegetables, has increased; thus in 1990 babies may be given more combined dishes rather than given meat, potatoes and vegetables as individual courses.

6.4 The consumption of meat in infancy

Meat is an important source of iron. The Department of Health recommends that babies should be given meat regularly. In 1990 mothers were asked for the first time whether they were giving meat to their baby and those who were not were asked why they were not doing so. Table 6.11 shows that nearly all (94%) of the babies had had meat by nine months of age, and over 90% of the babies in every social class group had had meat. However, Table 6.11 indicates that babies from the higher social class groups were more likely to have had meat than those from the lower social class groups (97% of babies in Social Class I had had meat, compared with 91% in Social Class V).

Table 6.11 Proportion of mothers who have given meat at nine months by social class as defined by current or last occupation of husband/partner (1990 Great Britain)

Social class	Percentage who have given meat at nine months	Base*:
I	97	397
II	95	1,047
IIINM	96	427
IIIM	94	1,608
IV	93	739
V	91	117
No partner	92	313
Unclassified	91	755
Total	94	5,404

All babies who were given solid food at nine months.

The last row in Table 6.12 shows that nearly all the babies who had ever had meat in 1990 were having meat at the nine months stage. This means that 93% of all the babies were having meat at the nine months stage. The table also reveals that meat was consumed frequently; the last column in Table 6.12 indicates that 40% of the babies had meat every day and 94% had meat at least once a week. Babies from every social class group ate meat frequently but again babies from the higher social class groups had meat more often than babies from the lower social class groups; 82% of the babies from Social Class I had meat at least three times a week while only 68% of babies in Social Class V and those whose mothers were not living with their husband/partner had meat at least three times a week.

Mothers of the 345 babies who were not having meat at the nine months stage were asked why they did not offer meat. Their reasons are presented in Table 6.13. The most com-

monly cited reason was that the baby was not ready to eat meat; 67% of the mothers who did not offer meat (5% of the 5,413 mothers in the sample) believed that their baby was not ready to eat meat at nine months. The second most often cited reason was that the mother intended to give the baby a vegetarian diet; 24% of the mothers who did not offer meat (2% of the whole sample) intended to give their baby a vegetarian diet.

There were clear social class differences in the reasons given by the 345 mothers who did not offer meat for not offering meat. Mothers in Social Classes I and II who did not offer meat tended to do so because they wanted their baby to have a vegetarian diet; 51% of mothers in Social Classes I and II who did not offer meat gave this reason while between 10% to 18% of the other groups cited vegetarianism as a reason for avoiding meat. Mothers from Social Classes III, IV, V and those not living with a partner or whose social class was unclassified tended not to offer meat because they felt that their baby was not ready for meat at the nine months stage; between 73% to 80% of the mothers in these groups who did not offer meat gave this reason while only 40% of mothers in Social Classes I and II said that their baby was not ready for meat. Mothers in these groups were also more likely than mothers in Social Classes I and II to say that they did not offer meat because their baby did not like meat (between 7% to 9% gave this reason compared with 5% in Social Classes I and II).

The Department of Health recommends that babies who do not eat meat should be given vitamin supplements to improve their ability to absorb iron present in vegetables. In 1990, only 26% of the 345 babies who were not having meat at the nine months

Table 6.12 Frequency in the consumption of meat at nine months by social class as defined by current or last occupation of husband/partner (1990 Great Britain)

Percentage having meat	Social class								Total
	I	II	IIINM	IIIM	IV	V	No partner	Unclassified	
Every day	42	40	41	40	40	36	38	35	40
At least three times a week	82	78	81	78	73	68	68	72	76
At least once a week	95	94	95	96	94	92	92	93	94
Less often than once a week	4	5	4	4	6	6	7	6	5
Baby not having meat at the moment	1	1	1	0	1	2	1	0	1
Base: All babies who had ever had meat	385	986	409	1,514	686	106	694	286	5,067

Table 6.13 Reasons for not offering meat by social class as defined by current or last occupation of husband/partner (1990 Great Britain)

Reason for not offering meat	Social class				Total
	I and II	IIINM and IIIM	IV	V, no partner, Unclassified	
	%	%	%	%	%
Baby does not like meat	5	9	9	7	8
Baby is not ready to eat meat	40	73	80	74	67
Baby given a vegetarian diet	51	18	10	17	24
Other reasons	5	3	5	2	4
	100	100	100	100	100
Base: All babies who had never had meat	77	116	53	99	345

Percentages do not add up to 100 as some mothers gave more than one reason.

stage had vitamin supplements directly or were breastfed by mothers who took vitamin supplements. Due to the small numbers of babies involved it was not possible to examine if there were social class differences in the intake of vitamins among babies who were not having meat. (The use of vitamins in general will be covered in a later section.)

6.5 Influences on the choice of solid food

In the second and third stage questionnaires mothers were asked what they took into account when deciding what solid food to give their baby. This was asked as an open question without any precodes or prompting and many mothers mentioned more than one factor. The answers have been grouped as being related to nutritional factors or not, and are shown in Table 6.14. Some mention was made of general nutrition by 25% of mothers who were giving solid food at stage 2 and by 43% at stage 3. This included fairly unspecific comments like 'balanced diet', 'calories', 'what his digestion can cope with' or 'food value'. Sugar content was the next most common consideration, with 21% of mothers mentioning this at stage 2 and 18% mentioning it at stage 3. Salt, vitamins and additives were mentioned by over 10% of mothers at each stage. Of the non-nutritional factors, variety was the most common thing mentioned; 31% of the mothers mentioned it in stage 2 and 35% mentioned it at stage 3. This included variety of tastes and textures, for example mothers liked foods that could be made up to different thickness or that the baby could chew.

Table 6.14 shows that, compared with 1985, the proportion of mothers mentioning nutritional factors in 1990 has contracted in general while the proportion mentioning non-nutritional factors has grown.

The third stage questionnaires went on to ask mothers if they avoided giving food which contained particular ingredients, and if so, why. When the baby was aged between nine to ten months 51% of mothers said that they avoided particular ingredients; the ingredients avoided are listed in Table 6.15. In 1990, as in 1985, when mothers said that they took sugar, salt or additives into account when deciding what food to give their baby it appears that they meant that they cut down on these things as these were the most commonly avoided. Compared with 1985 a larger proportion of mothers were avoiding salt and specific food stuffs; 45% avoided salt in 1990 compared with 35% in 1985 and 64% avoided specific foodstuffs in 1990 as opposed to 30% in 1985. A smaller proportion of mothers were avoiding the other ingredients listed in Table 6.15 in 1990 compared to 1985.

Table 6.16 shows that in 1990, as in 1985, the majority of the reasons given for avoiding particular ingredients were rather general, 47% of mothers who avoided certain ingredients said

Table 6.15 Ingredients avoided by mothers who gave solid food at nine months (1985 and 1990 Great Britain)

Ingredients avoided	1985	1990
	Percentage avoiding each ingredient	
Sugar	55	53
Salt	35	45
Additives	31	19
Colourings	21	11
Preservatives	11	5
Fat	10	8
Flavourings	5	3
Other additives	2	1
Specific foodstuffs	30	64
Other	1	0
Base:	*3,055**	*2,649**

Percentages do not add up to 100 as some mothers avoided more than one ingredient.
* Bases are the reweighted numbers.

Table 6.14 What mothers took into account when deciding what solid foods to give (1985 and 1990 Great Britain)

	Baby aged:			
	4-5 months		9-10 months	
	1985	1990	1985	1990
	Percentage mentioning each factor			
Nutritional factors				
Nutrition generally eg 'balanced diet', 'food value'	32	25	51	43
Sugar content	29	21	22	18
Additives	14	12	18	10
Vitamins	13	12	14	20
Salt content	12	11	11	13
Gluten content	8	9	1	1
Protein content	5	2	8	8
Fat content	4	2	8	8
Mineral content	1	2	2	6
Carbohydrate content	1	0	2	2
Non-nutritional factors				
Variety	30	31	27	35
Baby's preferences	21	24	19	25
Home cooked	5	9	7	17
Ease of preparation	5	9	4	8
Price	5	6	4	4
Baby's age	5	5	1	0
Other eg size of packet, shelf-life	20	38	12	57
Base:	4,591*	5,316*	4,733*	5,404*

Percentages do not add up to 100 as some mothers gave more than one reason.
* Bases are the reweighted numbers.

Table 6.16 Reasons for avoiding particular ingredients (1985 and 1990 Great Britain)

Reasons for avoiding particular ingredients	1985	1990
	Percentage giving reason	
Not beneficial	59	47
Harmful	30	33
Other problems	25	18
Bad for teeth	22	27
Hyperactivity	10	16
Allergies	12	16
Developed a sweet tooth	11	7
Publicity	9	8
Other reasons	14	7
Base:	*2,930**	*2,532**

Percentages do not add up to 100 as some mothers avoided more than one ingredient.
* Bases are the reweighted numbers.

it was because they thought they were not beneficial, and 33% said they thought the ingredients were harmful. Of the more specific reasons given, the most common was that it was 'bad for the teeth'; 27% gave this reason presumably for avoiding sugar. Thus it appears that about a quarter of all mothers are deliberately avoiding sugar as they feel it is not good for the baby particularly the teeth. *Present day practice in infant feeding; third report*[1] sees this as a desirable feeding practice as it states that 'when solid food are introduced, the regulation of sugar consumption is desirable so as to reduce the risk of dental caries and the possibility of obesity.'

Table 6.16 shows that, compared with 1985, mothers in 1990 placed more emphasis on the harmfulness of particular ingredients, the effect on teeth, hyperactivity and allergies. A larger proportion of mothers mentioned these reasons. In contrast, smaller proportions of mothers in 1990 than in 1985 listed the risk of developing a sweet tooth and ingredients not being beneficial as reasons for avoiding particular ingredients.

6.6 Additional drinks

At all stages of the survey mothers were asked whether or not they gave their baby any additional drinks apart from milk. In 1990 as in previous years, bottle fed babies were more likely to be given additional drinks than breastfed babies; Table 6.17 shows that 89% of bottle fed babies were given drinks compared with 58% of breastfed babies. Taking all babies together, 79% were given additional drinks in 1990, a decrease from 86% in 1985 and 88% in 1980. This decline occurred among both breast and bottle fed babies. Among breastfed babies the proportion dropped from 68% in 1985 to 58% in 1990 and the decline for bottle fed babies was from 94% in 1985 to 89% in 1990. The proportion of mothers giving breastfed babies drinks at six weeks has been falling since 1980 (Table 6.17) but the decline among bottle fed babies was only apparent since 1985. Moreover, the contraction between 1985 and 1990 was sharper among breastfed babies than among their bottle fed counterparts. Thus, despite the decline in the proportion of mothers giving non-milk drinks to both breast and bottle fed babies, the difference between the two groups has increased since 1985.

The Department of Health recommends that successful breastfeeding is facilitated by, among other approaches, avoiding additional drinks. It advises that mothers of bottle fed babies offer formula milk, which is nutritionally complete, in preference to other drinks. The decline in the proportion of mothers giving additional drinks at six weeks since 1985 (and 1980 among breastfed babies) is encouraging.

By the time the babies were around four months old the proportion receiving additional drinks in 1990 had risen to 88%. Bottle fed babies were still more likely than breastfed ones to have been given additional drinks; 92% compared with 74%. This was also the case in 1985. But by the time they were nine months old nearly all the babies (98%) were given drinks in additional to milk.

In 1990, as in 1985, mothers were asked at each stage to list the types of drinks they usually gave their baby. Their answers are set out in Table 6.18.

At six weeks the majority of mothers (59%) were giving their baby plain water. A considerable proportion (45%) were giving a herbal baby drink which contains sugar and 18% gave other baby drinks, the majority of which were unsweetened. Table 6.18 shows that compared with 1985 more mothers gave plain water or a herbal drink at six weeks, fewer gave other baby drinks and a much smaller proportion gave water with sugar or honey added. Compared with 1985 mothers in 1990 were more likely to give unsweetened drinks (74% compared with 61%) and were less likely to give sweetened drinks (50% compared with 74% in 1985). However, neither the 1985 nor the 1990 survey collected information on the volume of drinks consumed thus it is not known whether babies in 1990 were having less sweetened drinks when quantity is also taken into account.

The most common drinks given to the babies when they were four months old were herbal baby drinks which contain sugar and unsweetened baby drinks; the proportion of mothers giving each of these drinks was 49% (Table 6.18). Plain water was still a common drink at this stage; 31% of the mothers were giving plain water. Under a fifth (18%) were giving a

Table 6.17   Additional drinks given to babies at about six weeks by feeding method (1980, 1985 and 1990 Great Britain)

Whether additional drinks given at about six weeks	Breastfed			Bottle fed			All babies		
	1980	1985	1990	1980	1985	1990	1980	1985	1990
	%	%	%	%	%	%	%	%	%
Drinks given	76	68	58	95	94	89	88	86	79
No drinks given	24	32	42	5	6	11	12	14	21
	100	100	100	100	100	100	100	100	100
Base:	*1,520*	*1,719*	*1,764*	*2,704*	*3,504*	*3,649*	*4,224*	*5,223*	*5,413*

Table 6.29   Who usually looks after the baby while the mother is working (1985 and 1990 Great Britain)

Person who looked after the baby	Four months						Nine months					
	Breastfed		Bottle fed		All babies		Breastfed		Bottle fed		All babies	
	1985	1990	1985	1990	1985	1990	1985	1990	1985	1990	1985	1990
	%	%	%	%	%	%	%	%	%	%	%	%
Mother herself: homeworker	⎤	⎤	⎤	⎤	⎤	⎤	21	8	7	5	8	6
out to work	⎦17	⎦16	⎦9	⎦8	⎦11	⎦9	3	3	2	1	2	1
Mother's husband/partner	19	34	28	37	26	37	15	25	32	32	31	31
Mother's mother/mother-in-law	19	20	33	29	29	27	17	22	28	30	27	29
Child minder	23	22	18	17	19	18	31	29	20	24	21	24
Nursery/creche	1	1	1	2	1	2	-	7	2	3	2	3
Other	21	8	11	6	14	7	13	8	9	6	9	6
	100	100	100	100	100	100	100	100	100	100	100	100
Base:	*175†*	*194†*	*558†*	*905†*	*733†*	*1,099†*	*81†*	*160†*	*980†*	*1,660†*	*1,061†*	*1,820†*

† Bases are the reweighted numbers.

Table 6.29 also shows that husbands and partners have taken on a more prominent role in looking after the baby since 1985 (37% in 1990 looked after the baby while the mother was working compared with 26% in 1985). In contrast, the role played by facilities other than the mother herself, her relatives, childminders, nurseries and creches has become smaller; only 7% of mothers in 1990 used other facilities compared with 14% in 1985.

When the baby was nine months old the pattern of child care adopted by mothers in paid work was much the same as it had been at four months; breastfeeding mothers were less likely to have their mothers or mothers-in-law to look after the baby, 22% of breastfeeding mothers used their mothers or mothers-in-law while 30% of all mothers did so (Table 6.29). Breastfeeding mothers also had a slightly higher tendency to use childminders (29% compared with 24% of all mothers). The last two columns of Table 6.29 shows that compared with 1985, a larger proportion of mothers used childminders (24% compared with 21% in 1985), and a slightly smaller proportion looked after the baby themselves (6% compared with 8% in 1985).

When the babies were about nine months old breastfeeding mothers were just as likely as bottle feeding mothers to pay for child care, 61% in both cases. Mothers in paid employment who were still breastfeeding when the baby was about nine months old were asked how they usually fed their baby while they were at work. The majority, 39% said that the baby had other milk while they were at work, 6% said they were able to take the baby with them to work, 4% expressed breast milk for the baby and the remainder had other arrangements.

Reference

[1] *Present day practice in infant feeding: third report.* Report on Health and Social Subjects 32. DHSS (1988).

7 Infant feeding practices in England and Wales, Scotland and Northern Ireland

7.1 Introduction

The 1990 survey covered Northern Ireland for the first time. It is the first opportunity to compare infant feeding practices in England and Wales with those in both Scotland and Northern Ireland. Figures for the United Kingdom are little different than those for Great Britain, as the actual number of births in Northern Ireland are a small proportion of those in the United Kingdom as a whole. When the data are weighted to take account of the actual number of births occuring in each country, even where the practices are very different in Northern Ireland than in Great Britain it has little impact on the overall picture.

7.2 Incidence of breastfeeding

As stated earlier in this report, incidence of breastfeeding is defined as the proportion of babies who were put to the breast at all, even if this was on one occasion only. Table 7.1 shows that the incidence of breastfeeding in Northern Ireland, at 36%, is substantially lower than for the other countries of the United Kingdom - England and Wales at 64% and Scotland at 50%. While this may be because of social and cultural differences between the countries, or differences in policy and practice between health professionals, it could also be because of different demographic structures in the countries. It has been demonstrated in this report and the earlier surveys that both birth order and social class are strongly associated with rates of breastfeeding, so we next examine whether all or part of the difference between the countries is due to either of these factors.

7.2.1 Incidence of breastfeeding and birth order

This survey has supported the findings of previous surveys that the highest incidence of breastfeeding is found among first babies. Northern Ireland proves no exception, here the incidence of breastfeeding among first births is 42%, compared with 32% for second and subsequent births. First births in Northern Ireland, however, are a lower proportion of all births, at 38%, than in either England and Wales (45%) or Scotland (48%). We therefore examined rates of breastfeeding within the three countries for first births and later births. As Table 7.2 shows, Northern Ireland has the lowest incidence of breastfeeding among mothers having their first child, 42% of whom ever breastfed compared with 70% in England and Wales and 56% in Scotland. Among mothers having their

Table 7.1   Incidence of breastfeeding by country (1990 United Kingdom)

Method of feeding at birth	England and Wales	Scotland	Northern Ireland	United Kingdom
	%	%	%	%
Breast	64	50	36	62
Bottle	36	50	64	38
	100	100	100	100
Base:	4,942*	1,981*	1,497*	5,533†

* Weighted by social class to give a national estimate.
† Weighted by social class and region to give a United Kingdom estimate.

Table 7.2   Incidence of breastfeeding by birth order (1990 United Kingdom)

Birth order	England and Wales	Scotland	Northern Ireland	United Kingdom
	Percentage breastfeeding at birth			
First birth	70	56	42	68
Second or later births	59	45	32	57
All babies	64	50	36	62
Bases*:				
First birth	2,204	949	567	2,475
Second or later births	2,738	1,032	930	3,058
All babies	4,942	1,981	1,497	5,533

* Weighted by social class to give a national estimate.
† Weighted by social class and region to give a United Kingdom estimate.

second or later children, 32% of Northern Ireland mothers breastfed, compared with 59% in England and Wales and 45% in Scotland.

7.2.2 Incidence of breastfeeding and social class

As we have seen in earlier chapters, social class is also strongly associated with the incidence of breastfeeding, and the distribution of social class is different for England and Wales, Scotland and Northern Ireland. As Table 7.3 shows, the pattern of lower rates of breastfeeding in Northern Ireland held for every social class group, except for Social Class I, where the incidence of breastfeeding was above 80% for all the countries, and was only marginally lower in Northern Ireland (81%) than in Scotland (84%) and England and Wales (87%).

7.3 Prevalence of breastfeeding

Prevalence of breastfeeding is the proportion of babies still being breastfed at specified ages, whether or not they were also receiving bottles or solid food. As Table 7.4 shows, the prevalence of breastfeeding in Northern Ireland is lower at all ages than it is in either England and Wales or Scotland. By the time the baby was two weeks old, only 27% of mothers in Northern Ireland were breastfeeding, compared with over half (51%) in England and Wales and 39% in Scotland. By six weeks after the birth, breastfeeding had fallen to 17% in Northern Ireland. Less than a tenth of babies in Northern Ireland were being breastfed by the age of four months.

7.4 Duration of breastfeeding

As mothers in Northern Ireland were less likely to breastfeed in the first place it is hardly surprising that the prevalence of breastfeeding at different ages is much lower than in the rest of the United Kingdom. In order to establish the length of time for which mothers in the different countries breastfed we need to look separately at those mothers who breastfed at all. Table 7.5 relates only to those mothers who started breastfeeding at all, and shows how long they continued to breastfeed, whether or not they were also giving other foods.

Table 7.3 Incidence of breastfeeding by social class as defined by current or last occupation of husband/partner (1990 United Kingdom)

Social class	England and Wales	Scotland	Northern Ireland	United Kingdom
	Percentage breastfeeding at birth			
I	87	84	81	86
II	80	72	51	79
IIINM	74	61	44	72
IIIM	60	47	33	58
IV	55	40	33	53
V	42	28	18	40
Unclassified	62	50	34	60
No partner	45	23	17	42
Bases:				
I	*365*	*139*	*67*	*403*
II	*965*	*364*	*283*	*1,074*
IIINM	*390*	*159*	*109*	*436*
IIIM	*1,475*	*573*	*446*	*1,647*
IV	*674*	*264*	*136*	*747*
V	*103*	*58*	*66*	*122*
Unclassified	*284*	*124*	*122*	*323*
No partner	*688*	*301*	*271*	*781*

* Bases for the United Kingdom are weighted by social class and region. All other bases are weighted by social class only.

Table 7.4 Prevalence of breastfeeding at ages up to nine months by country (1990 United Kingdom)

Age of baby	England and Wales	Scotland	Northern Ireland	United Kingdom
	Percentage breastfeeding at each age			
Birth	64	50	36	62
1 week	54	41	29	53
2 weeks	51	39	27	50
6 weeks	39	30	17	39
4 months	25	20	8	25
6 months	21	16	5	21
9 months	12	9	3	11
Base:	*4,942**	*1,981**	*1,497**	*5,533†*

* Weighted by social class to give a national estimate.
† Weighted by social class and region to give a United Kingdom estimate.

Table 7.5 Duration of breastfeeding in the United Kingdom by country (1990)

	England and Wales	Scotland	Northern Ireland	United Kingdom
	Percentage still breastfeeding			
Birth	100	100	100	100
1 week	85	83	81	85
2 weeks	80	77	75	80
6 weeks	62	60	49	61
4 months	39	39	23	39
6 months	33	33	15	33
9 months	18	19	8	18
Base:	*3,149**	*994**	*531**	*3,438†*

* *Weighted by social class to give a national estimate.*
† *Weighted by social class and region to give a United Kingdom estimate.*

As the table clearly shows, mothers in Northern Ireland who breastfed at all did so for a shorter time than those in England and Wales and Scotland. By the time the baby was two weeks old the differences were slight, with 80% in England and Wales still breastfeeding, compared with 77% in Scotland and 75% in Northern Ireland. By six weeks after the birth, however, 62% of women in England and Wales who initially breastfed were continuing to do so, compared with 60% in Scotland and less than half, 49%, in Northern Ireland. By the time the baby was four months of age, 39% of breastfeeding mothers in England, Wales and Scotland were still breastfeeding, but in Northern Ireland the proportion was 23%. Just under a fifth of breastfed babies were still being breastfed at nine months in England and Wales (18%) and Scotland (19%), compared with under a tenth (8%) of breastfed babies in Northern Ireland.

7.5 Age of introduction of solid food.

Table 7.6 shows the age at which mothers in the countries of the United Kingdom first introduced their babies to solid food.

The differences between England and Wales, Scotland and Northern Ireland are relatively slight, with the tendency being for Scottish mothers to introduce solid food earliest, followed by those in Northern Ireland, with the English and Welsh mothers introducing them latest. The greatest difference was at the eight week stage, by which time 19% of Scottish mothers had introduced their baby to solids, as had 18% of mothers in Northern Ireland, but only 12% of those in England and Wales.

7.6 Additional drinks

As Table 7.7 shows, mothers in Northern Ireland were more likely than those in England, Wales and Scotland to give additional drinks, as well as milk, to their babies at about six weeks old. Eighty six per cent of them did so, compared with 79% in both England and Wales and Scotland.

At around four months of age, the babies in Northern Ireland were still more likely than their counterparts in England Wales and Scotland to be receiving drinks in addition to milk. Again, the percentage doing so in England and Wales (88%) and

Table 7.6 Age at introduction of solid food by country (1990 United Kingdom)

Age at introduction of solid food	England and Wales	Scotland	Northern Ireland	United Kingdom
	Percentage giving solid food			
4 weeks	2	3	3	3
6 weeks	6	10	11	7
8 weeks	12	19	18	13
3 months	53	58	56	53
4 months	83	83	81	83
6 months	96	96	95	96
9 months	100	100	100	100
Base:	*4,942**	*1,981**	*1,497**	*5,533†*

* *Weighted by social class to give a national estimate.*
† *Weighted by social class and region to give a United Kingdom estimate.*

Table 7.7 Whether drinks other than milk were given at six weeks and at four months by country (1990 United Kingdom)

Drinks given other than milk	England and Wales	Scotland	Northern Ireland	United Kingdom
	Percentage giving drinks			
At six weeks	79	79	86	79
At four months	88	88	94	88
Base:	*4,942**	*1,981**	*1,497**	*5,533†*

* *Weighted by social class to give a national estimate.*
† *Weighted by social class and region to give a United Kingdom estimate.*

Table 7.8   Whether baby was given extra vitamins at six weeks and at four months by country (1990 United Kingdom)

Extra vitamins given	England and Wales	Scotland	Northern Ireland	United Kingdom
	Percentage giving extra vitamins			
At six weeks	11	21	6	12
At four months	18	28	21	19
Base:	*4,942**	*1,981**	*1,497**	*5,533†*

* *Weighted by social class to give a national estimate.*
† *Weighted by social class and region to give a United Kingdom estimate.*

Scotland (88%) was identical, while in Northern Ireland 94% were receiving additional drinks.

In Northern Ireland, as in the mainland countries, there was an association between giving additional drinks and the method by which the baby was fed. Among breastfed babies 64% had additional drinks at 6 weeks, compared with 89% of those who were entirely bottle fed and 87% of those who were fed by both breast and bottle.

7.7 Supplementary vitamins

As Table 7.8 shows, mothers in Northern Ireland were the least likely to give supplementary vitamins when the baby was six weeks old. Only 6% did so, compared with 11% in England and Wales and 21% in Scotland. By four months of age, the differences were less noticeable. Among Northern Ireland mothers 21% were giving supplementary vitamins, a similar figure to the 18% giving them in England and Wales, and slightly lower than the 28% of Scottish mothers giving vitamin supplements.

Appendices

Appendix I Composition of the 1990 sample compared with the 1985 sample and with the 1990 population estimates

Table I.1 Distribution of the population and the sample by birth order (1980, 1985 and 1990 Great Britain)

Birth order	Population*			Surveys		
	1980	1985	1990	1980	1985	1990
	%	%	%	%	%	%
First birth	43	40	40	44	46	45
Second birth	36	36	37	36	33	32
Third birth	14	16	16	13	14	16
Fourth birth	⌝7	⌝8	⌝8	5⌝7	5⌝7	5⌝8
Fifth or later birth				2⌟	2⌟	3⌟
	100	100	100	100	100	100
Base:	*601,600*	*584,500*	*554,200*	*4,224*	*5,223*	*5,413*

* *Figures bases on legitimate live births only.*

Table I.2 Distribution of the sample by mother's main occupation (1980, 1985 and 1990 Great Britain)

Main occupation	1980	1985	1990
	%	%	%
Professional	1	1	2
Teaching	6	5	3
Nursing, medical or social	8	7	6
Other managerial or intermediate non-manual	5	6	6
Clerical	34	28	28
Shop assistant or related sales	7	9	13
Total non-manual	**61**	**55**	**58**
Skilled manual	9	6	7
Semi-skilled factory work	12	12	14
Semi-skilled domestic work	3	5	6
Other semi-skilled	2	2	2
Unskilled	1	1	2
Total manual	**27**	**26**	**31**
Not classified	12	18	10
	100	100	100
Base:	*4,224*	*5,223*	*5,413*

Table I.3 Distribution of the population and the sample by social class as defined by current or last occupation of husband/partner (1980, 1985 and 1990 Great Britain)

Social class	Surveys All births			Population*		
	1980	1985	1990	1980	1985	1990
	%	%	%	%	%	%
I & II	26	26	26	25	24	25
IIINM	8	8	8	10	9	8
All non-manual	34	34	34	35	33	33
IIIM	42	32	30	32	28	24
IV & V	16	19	16	18	16	12
All manual	58	51	46	50	44	36
Unclassified	]8	4]15	6]17	3	4	3
No husband/partner		11]	14]	..	..	..
Illegitimate†	..	..	..	12	19	28
	100	100	100	100	100	100
Base:	4,224	5,223	5,413	725,000	723,000	772,100

* Figures bases on live births in Great Britain in 1985 and 1990.
† Births to unmarried mothers.

Note: Due to differences in definitions, the survey figures for births to mothers with no husband/partner are not directly comparable to the population figures for illegitimate births.

Table I.4 Distribution of the sample by age at which another completed full-time education, for first and later births (1980, 1985 and 1990 Great Britain)

Age at which mother completed full-time education	First births			Later births			All babies*		
	1980	1985	1990	1980	1985	1990	1980	1985	1990
	%	%	%	%	%	%	%	%	%
16 or under	59	56	49	66	63	57	63	60	54
17 or 18	25	30	35	19	23	30	21	26	32
Over 18	16	14	16	15	14	13	16	14	14
	100	100	100	100	100	100	100	100	100
Base:	1,831	2,347	2,430	2,337	2,875	2,983	4,224	5,223	5,413

* Includes some cases for whom the exact birth order was not known.

Table I.5 Distribution of social class as defined by current or last occupation of husband/partner by age at which mother finished full-time education (1980, 1985 and 1990 Great Britain)

Social class	Mother's age at finishing full-time education											
	16 or under			17 or 18			Over 18			All ages*		
	1980	1985	1990	1980	1985	1990	1980	1985	1990	1980	1985	1990
	%	%	%	%	%	%	%	%	%	%	%	%
I	3	2	4	8	7	6	29	21	23	8	6	7
II	12	12	13	23	24	22	38	46	38	18	20	20
IIINM	8	8	6	11	11	11	9	8	9	8	8	8
Total non-manual	**22**	**21**	**23**	**42**	**42**	**39**	**76**	**75**	**70**	**34**	**34**	**35**
IIIM	49	37	34	40	31	31	16	13	15	42	32	30
IV	16	17	16	10	13	13	3	6	5	13	14	14
V	4	6	3	2	4	2	-	-	-	3	5	2
Total manual	**69**	**60**	**53**	**52**	**48**	**46**	**19**	**19**	**18**	**58**	**51**	**46**
Unclassified	..]9	5]19	6]24	..]6	2]10	6]15	..]5	4]6	5]11	..]8	4]15	6]20
No partner	..	14]	18]	..	8]	10]	..	3]	6]	..	11]	14]
	100	100	100	100	100	100	100	100	100	100	100	100
Base:	2,632	3,110	2,880	892	1,346	1,710	657	725	775	4,224	5,223	5,413

* Includes some cases for whom the age at finishing full-time education was not known.

Table I.6   Distribution of the population and the sample by mother's age (1980, 1985 and 1990 Great Britain)

Mother's age	Population*			Surveys		
	1980	1985	1990	1980	1985	1990
	%	%	%	%	%	%
Under 20	9	9	8	8	8	7
20-24	31	30	26	31	30	25
25-29	34	35	36	36	35	37
30 or over	26	27	31	25	27	31
	100	100	100	100	100	100
Base:	725,000	723,100	772,073	4,224	5,223	5,413

* Figures bases on all live births.

Table I.7   Distribution of the sample of mother's age, for first and later births (1980, 1985 and 1990 Great Britain)

Mother's age	First births			Later births			All babies*		
	1980	1985	1990	1980	1985	1990	1980	1985	1990
	%	%	%	%	%	%	%	%	%
Under 20	15	16	13	2	2	2	8	8	7
20-24	40	38	31	24	23	20	31	30	25
25-29	33	31	36	38	38	39	36	35	37
30 or over	12	14	20	36	38	39	25	27	31
	100	100	100	100	100	100	100	100	100
Base:	1,831	2,347	2,430	2,377	2,875	2,983	4,224	5,223	5,413

* Includes some cases for whom the exact birth order was not known.

Table I.8   Age of mothers of first babies by social class as defined by current or last occupation of husband/partner (1980, 1985 and 1990 Great Britain)

Mother's age	Social class														
	I			II			IIINM			IIIM			IV and V		
	1980	1985	1990	1980	1985	1990	1980	1985	1990	1980	1985	1990	1980	1985	1990
	%	%	%	%	%	%	%	%	%	%	%	%	%	%	%
Under 20	-	2	4	3	3	2	4	4	9	15	10	11	23	22	18
20-24	15	16	14	27	25	21	33	33	30	50	46	34	48	47	44
25-29	52	49	47	51	42	45	49	44	41	27	34	39	21	24	27
30 or over	33	32	36	19	30	33	14	19	21	8	9	16	8	8	11
	100	100	100	100	100	100	100	100	100	100	100	100	100	100	100
Base:	138	136	191	311	444	447	179	213	201	742	703	684	266	386	346

Table I.9   Age of mothers of first babies at finishing full-time education (1980, 1985 and 1990 Great Britain)

Mother's age	Age at which mother finished full-time education								
	16 or under			17 or 18			Over 18		
	1980	1985	1990	1980	1985	1990	1980	1985	1990
	%	%	%	%	%	%	%	%	%
Under 20	21	23	20	11	10	9	-	0	1
20-24	44	42	35	44	42	33	21	15	15
25-29	26	25	31	35	35	41	56	47	44
30 or over	9	9	14	10	13	18	23	37	40
	100	100	100	100	100	100	100	100	100
Base:	1,067	1,309	1,183	453	697	837	298	328	387

Table I.10   Distribution of the sample by region (1980, 1985 and 1990 Great Britain)

Region	1980	1985	1990
	%	%	%
London and South East	30	32	33
South West and Wales	11	13	12
Midlands and East Anglia	19	18	19
North	30	26	27
Scotland	11	11	9
	100	100	100
Base:	*4,224*	*5,223*	*5,413*

Table I.11   Distribution of birth order by region (1980, 1985 and 1990 Great Britain)

Birth order	Region														
	London and South East			South West and Wales			Midlands and East Anglia			North			Scotland*		
	1980	1985	1990	1980	1985	1990	1980	1985	1990	1980	1985	1990	1980	1985	1990
	%	%	%	%	%	%	%	%	%	%	%	%	%	%	%
First birth	45	45	45	41	45	42	43	44	43	44	46	48	42	46	48
Second and subsequent birth	55	55	55	59	55	58	57	56	57	56	54	52	58	54	52
	100	100	100	100	100	100	100	100	100	100	100	100	100	100	100
Base:	*138*	*136*	*191*	*311*	*444*	*447*	*179*	*213*	*201*	*742*	*703*	*684*	*266*	*386*	*346*

Table I.12   Distribution of social class as defined by current or last occupation of husband/partner by region (1980, 1985 and 1990 Great Britain)

Social class	Region														
	London and South East			South West and Wales			Midlands and East Anglia			North			Scotland*		
	1980	1985	1990	1980	1985	1990	1980	1985	1990	1980	1985	1990	1980	1985	1990
	%	%	%	%	%	%	%	%	%	%	%	%	%	%	%
I	11	8	9	9	6	7	5	4	6	6	4	6	8	6	7
II	22	25	24	15	19	20	19	18	16	16	16	16	16	16	18
IIINM	9	9	9	9	9	8	8	6	6	8	9	8	7	9	8
Total non-manual	42	42	42	33	34	36	32	28	28	30	29	30	31	32	33
IIIM	38	30	28	43	32	32	44	38	33	44	30	29	41	33	29
IV	9	10	10	16	15	14	13	17	17	14	17	16	15	13	13
V	2	4	2	2	5	1	2	3	2	4	6	3	5	7	3
Total manual	49	43	39	61	52	47	59	58	51	62	53	48	61	53	45
Unclassified	.. ⌉9	4 ⌉14	6 ⌉18	.. ⌉6	3 ⌉14	7 ⌉17	.. ⌉9	4 ⌉15	6 ⌉20	.. ⌉8	4 ⌉18	5 ⌉22	.. ⌉8	3 ⌉15	6 ⌉22
No partner	.. ⌋	10 ⌋	13 ⌋	.. ⌋	10 ⌋	10 ⌋	.. ⌋	10 ⌋	15 ⌋	.. ⌋	13 ⌋	17 ⌋	.. ⌋	12 ⌋	15 ⌋
	100	100	100	100	100	100	100	100	100	100	100	100	100	100	100
Base:	*1,284*	*1,675*	*1,785*	*483*	*657*	*606*	*808*	*960*	*1,040*	*1,179*	*1,378*	*1,452*	*1,718*	*1,895*	*1,981*

* The data for Scotland are weighted to give a national estimate.

Table I.13 Distribution of mother's age at finishing full-time education by region (1980, 1985 and 1990 Great Britain)

Mother's age at finishing full-time education	Region														
	London and South East			South West and Wales			Midlands and East Anglia			North			Scotland*		
	1980	1985	1990	1980	1985	1990	1980	1985	1990	1980	1985	1990	1980	1985	1990
	%	%	%	%	%	%	%	%	%	%	%	%	%	%	%
16 or under	55	52	45	61	55	48	67	64	62	69	69	61	65	63	54
17 or 18	25	29	35	25	31	37	19	26	29	18	21	29	19	23	29
Over 18	20	19	20	14	14	15	14	10	9	13	11	10	16	14	17
	100	100	100	100	100	100	100	100	100	100	100	100	100	100	100
Base:	*1,284*	*1,662*	*1,762*	*483*	*654*	*663*	*808*	*950*	*1,035*	*1,179*	*1,364*	*1,438*	*1,718*	*1,895*	*1,981*

* *The data for Scotland are weighted to give a national estimate.*
† *Excludes some cases for whom the age at finishing full-time education was not known.*

Table II.1 Distribution of the sample by birth order and country (1990 United Kingdom

Birth order	England and Wales	Scotland	Northern Ireland
	%	%	%
First birth	45	48	38
Second birth	32	31	29
Third birth	16	14	17
Fourth birth	5	5	8
Fifth or later births	2	2	8
	100	100	100
Base:	*4,942*	*1,981*	*1,498*

Table II.2 Distribution of the sample by mother's age, birth order and country (1990 United Kingdom)

Mother's age	First births								
	England and Wales	Scotland	Northern Ireland	England and Wales	Scotland	Northern Ireland	England and Wales	Scotland	Northern Ireland
	%	%	%	%	%	%	%	%	%
Under 20	13	11	15	2	2	2	7	6	7
20-24	31	32	34	20	19	18	25	25	24
25-29	36	37	35	38	40	36	37	38	36
30 and over	20	20	15	40	39	44	31	30	33
	100	100	100	100	100	100	100	100	100
Base:	*2,204*	*950*	*568*	*2,738*	*1,031*	*930*	*4,942*	*1,981*	*1,498*

Table II.3 Distribution of the sample by social class as defined by current or last occupation of husband/partner and country (1990 United Kingdom

Social class	England and Wales	Scotland	Northern Ireland
	%	%	%
I	7	7	4
II	20	18	19
IIINM	8	8	7
Total Non-manual	**35**	**33**	**30**
IIIM	30	29	30
IV	14	13	9
V	2	3	4
Total Manual	**46**	**45**	**43**
Unclassified	6	6	8
No partner	14	15	18
	100	100	100
Base:	*4,942*	*1,981*	*1,497*

Table II.4 Distribution of the sample by age at which mother completed full-time education, birth order and country (1990 United Kingdom)

Age at which mother completed full-time education	First births								
	England and Wales	Scotland	Northern Ireland	England and Wales	Scotland	Northern Ireland	England and Wales	Scotland	Northern Ireland
	%	%	%	%	%	%	%	%	%
16 or under	49	50	38	57	58	46	54	54	43
17 or 18	35	31	43	30	28	38	32	29	40
19 or over	16	19	20	13	15	16	14	17	18
	100	100	100	100	100	100	100	100	100
Base:	*2,204*	*950*	*568*	*2,738*	*1,031*	*930*	*4,942*	*1,981*	*1,498*

Appendix III Sampling errors

Like all estimates based on samples, the results of the survey are subject to chance variations and errors in the results. For example, the sampling frame may be incomplete, questions might be interpreted in slightly different ways by different respondents, or respondents may for some reason give incorrect answers to questions. Error may be introduced when the data are coded or input to the computer. In this survey extensive efforts have been made to keep such errors to a minimum, including careful checking of the work of editing and coding staff.

Another potential source of error is response bias. Respondents to the survey, and those who respond to different stages of the survey, may differ in some respects from non-respondents, and so may not form a representative sample. For this survey steps have been taken to reduce error from this source by weighting the data in respect of variables where there is a known difference between respondents and the population.

A further source of error arises from the fact that estimates are based not on the whole population, but only a sample of it. There may be chance variations between such a sample and the whole population. These variations depend on both the size of the sample and its design. The standard error is a measure of the accuracy of a given proportion. Used in combination with the sample estimate it allows us to construct an interval, within which we can be confident, to a predetermined level, that the average result of all possible samples would fall. Ninety-five percent of the intervals from two standard errors below the estimate to two standard errors above the estimate would contain the average value of all possible samples. Such intervals are known as 95% confidence intervals. For example, the 95% confidence interval for the incidence of breast feeding in the whole sample, calculated on the figures below, is between 60.8% and 64.7%. In other words, there is a one in twenty chance that the true percentage of the population falls outside of these limits.

The tables below also show the design factors (defts) for the survey estimates. The design factor is the ratio of the standard error of the estimate in a complex sample to the standard error that the estimate would have had if a simple random sample of the same size had been used.

The tables also show the standard errors and defts for certain key variables in the report, categorised by demographic groups, in Table 1 for Great Britain and in Table 2 for the United Kingdom. The bases shown here may not correspond with those in the text, where full bases are given for consistency. Those shown below exclude cases where values for one or more of the variables were missing.

Table III.1 Standard errors for Great Britain, 1990

		Incidence	Standard error	Deft	Base
Incidence of breastfeeding:					
Total sample		63%	0.98	1.80	5413
Social class	I	86%	1.73	1.14	398
	II	79%	1.29	1.17	1052
	IIINM	73%	2.10	1.12	427
	IIIM	59%	1.38	1.30	1611
	IV & V	52%	1.90	1.39	853
	Unclassified & no partner	48%	1.60	1.44	1073
Region	London & South East	74%	1.45	1.48	1785
	South West & Wales	65%	3.59	2.09	666
	Midlands & East Anglia	59%	1.97	1.39	1040
	North	55%	2.25	1.87	1452
	Scotland	50%	1.09	1.03	1980
Mother's age	Under 20	39%	2.83	1.38	315
(mothers of first	20-24	61%	1.80	1.27	756
babies only)	25-29	77%	1.45	1.23	874
	30 and over	86%	1.36	1.01	479
Age at which mother	16 or under	50%	1.08	1.43	2880
finished full time	17 or 18	71%	1.41	1.52	1710
education	19 or over	91%	0.89	1.02	775
Birth order	First birth	69%	1.13	1.47	2430
	Later birth	58%	1.15	1.53	2983
Percentage of women who continued to breastfeed for at least 6 weeks after the birth:					
Total sample		62%	0.95	1.32	3351
Social class	I	78%	2.15	1.09	342
	II	71%	1.81	1.23	822
	IIINM	65%	2.73	1.13	308
	IIIM	57%	1.44	1.00	941
	IV & V	51%	2.29	1.14	430
	Unclassified & no partner	53%	2.31	1.36	507
Region	London & South East	67%	1.60	1.29	1301
	South West & Wales	70%	2.40	1.15	428
	Midlands & East Anglia	56%	2.11	1.12	604
	North	54%	2.13	1.27	783
	Scotland	60%	1.53	1.01	988
Age at which mother	16 or under	52%	1.33	1.17	1423
finished full time	17 or 18	63%	1.46	1.21	1201
education	19 or over	79%	1.64	1.26	699
Birth order	First birth	57%	1.34	1.14	1649
	Later birth	66%	1.14	1.29	1702
Percentage of women who gave additional drinks to the baby at around six weeks:					
Total sample		79%	0.68	1.49	5382
Method of feeding	Breast	58%	1.09	1.07	1750
	Bottle	89%	0.53	1.27	3631
Percentage of women who gave vitamins to the baby at around six weeks of age:					
Total sample		12%	0.77	2.09	5333
Percentage of women who had given solid food to the baby by 3 months:					
Total sample		68%	0.65	1.15	5230
Social class	I	57%	2.69	1.17	385
	II	61%	1.71	1.21	1007
	IIINM	70%	2.27	1.09	412
	IIIM	69%	1.26	1.18	1556
	IV & V	73%	1.54	1.16	841
	Unclassified & no partner	74%	1.23	1.12	1028
Region	London & South East	59%	1.08	0.90	1665
	South West & Wales	67%	2.44	1.32	641
	Midlands & East Anglia	72%	1.31	0.94	1028
	North	74%	1.27	1.12	1437
	Scotland	76%	1.01	1.03	1924
Percentage of women who gave vitamins to the baby at around four months of age:					
Total sample		19%	0.94	1.99	5383

Table III.2   Standard errors for United Kingdom 1990

		Incidence	Standard error	Deft	*Base*
Incidence of breastfeeding:					
Total sample		62%	0.95	1.95	*5533*
Social class	I	86%	1.71	1.20	*403*
	II	79%	1.27	1.25	*1074*
	IIINM	72%	2.06	1.20	*436*
	IIIM	58%	1.35	1.40	*1647*
	IV & V	51%	1.86	1.49	*869*
	Unclassified & no partner	47%	1.55	1.61	*1104*
Birth order	First birth	68%	1.11	1.58	*2475*
	Later birth	57%	1.13	1.67	*3058*
Percentage of women who continued to breastfeed for at least 6 weeks after the birth:					
Total sample		61%	0.94	1.39	*3393*
Percentage of women who gave additional drinks to the baby at around six weeks:					
Total sample		79%	0.68	1.62	*5382*
Percentage of women who gave vitamins to the baby at around six weeks of age:					
Total sample		12%	0.77	2.27	*5333*
Percentage of women who had given solid food to the baby by 3 months:					
Total sample		68%	0.64	1.25	*5346*
Percentage of women who gave vitamins to the baby at around four months of age:					
Total sample		19%	0.92	2.17	*5501*

Appendix IV   Survey documents

Five versions of the questionnaire were used, of which three are included here:

(a)   the original questionnaire sent to all mothers at six weeks (stage 1).

(b)   the questionnaire sent at four months to mothers who had been breastfeeding at the time of completing the first questionnaire (stage 2).

(c)   the questionnaire sent at nine months to mothers who had been breastfeeding at the time of completing the second questionnaire (stage 3).

Those questionnaires not included here differed from the others only in questions omitted.

Eighteen different covering letters were used according to the stage of the survey, whether it was the initial approach or a reminder, and depending on whether the baby was born in England and Wales, Scotland or Northern Ireland. Three of the letters are included here:

(a) the initial letter at six weeks
(b) the initial letter at four months
(c) the initial letter at nine months

Stage 1 questionnaire

OFFICE USE ONLY
N1299/1

| STAGE | 14 |

| BREAST = 1 | 15 |
| BOTTLE = 2 | |

| OUTCOME | 16/17 |

SURVEY OF INFANT FEEDING

1. Most questions on the following pages can be answered simply by putting a tick in the box next to the answer that applies to you.

   Example:

   Yes ☑ 1

   No ☐ 2

   Sometimes you are asked to write in a number or the answer in your own words. Please enter numbers as figures rather than words.

2. Occasionally you may have more than 1 answer to a question. Please tick all the boxes next to the answers that apply to you if the instruction "PLEASE TICK ONE OR MORE BOXES" is printed on top of the boxes.

3. Usually after answering each question you go on to the next one unless a box you have ticked has an arrow next to it with an instruction to go to another question

   Example:

   Yes ☑ 1 ——► Q5

   No ☐ 2

   By following the arrows carefully you will miss out some questions which do not apply to you, so the amount you have to fill in will make the questionnaire shorter than it looks.

4. If you cannot remember, do not know, or are unable to answer a particular question please write that in.

5. If, rather than a single baby, you have twins or triplets, please answer the questions in relation to the one who was born first.

6. When you have finished please post the questionnaire to us as soon as possible in the reply-paid envelope provided, even if you were not able to answer all of it.

The names and addresses of people who co-operate in surveys are held in strict confidence by OPCS and never passed to any other Government Department, or to members of the public or press.

We shall be very grateful for your help

If for any reason your baby is no longer with you please tick the box below and return the questionnaire to us so we do not trouble you you further.

My baby is no longer with me ☐

87

FIRST OF ALL WE WOULD LIKE TO ASK SOME GENERAL QUESTIONS BEFORE FINDING OUT HOW YOU FEED YOUR BABY AT PRESENT.

Please do not write in this column

1   What is your baby's first or Christian name? (Please write in below 1 letter per box)   [ ][ ][ ][ ][ ][ ][ ][ ][ ][ ]   18-32

2   How old is your baby?   PLEASE ENTER NUMBERS IN BOTH BOXES   [ ] weeks and [ ] days   33-34   35

3   Is your baby a boy or a girl?   Boy [1]   Girl [2]   36

4   Is this your first baby?   Yes [1]   No [2]   37

5   Is your baby one of twins or triplets?   No, neither [1]   Yes, twin [2]   Yes, triplet [3]

IF YOU HAVE TWINS OR TRIPLETS PLEASE COMPLETE THIS QUESTIONNAIRE WITH RESPECT TO THE ONE THAT WAS BORN FIRST   38

6   At the moment is your baby . . . . .   breast fed [1] →(a)   bottle fed [2] →Q7   or both? [3] →Q10   39

(a)   Do you give your baby milk in a bottle at present (apart from expressed breast milk)?   Yes (even if only occasionally) [1] →Q10   No [2] →Q14   40

1

7.   Did you ever put your baby to the breast?   Yes (even if it was once only) [1] →Q8   No, never [2] →Q10   41

8.   (a)   How old was your baby when you last breast fed him/her?   PLEASE ENTER AGE IN THE APPROPRIATE BOX:
EITHER [ ] days   OR [ ] weeks and [ ] days   42-43   44-45   46

(a)   What were your reasons for stopping breast feeding? (Please give all your reasons and explain)

MC=5   47-48   49-50   51-52   53-54   55-56

9.   Would you like to have continued breast feeding for longer or had you breast fed for as long as you intended?
Would have liked to have breast fed longer [1]
I have breast fed for as long as intended [2]   57

2

10. Which kind of milk do you give your baby most of the time at the moment?

PLEASE TICK ONE BOX ONLY

Cow and Gate Premium (powder)	01
Cow and Gate Premium (ready-to-feed)	02
Cow and Gate Plus (powder)	03
Cow and Gate Plus (ready-to-feed)	04
Cow and Gate Formula S (powder)	05
Ostermilk Two (powder)	06
Ostersoy (powder)	07
SMA Gold Cap (powder)	08
SMA Gold Cap (ready-to-feed)	09
SMA White Cap (powder)	10
SMA White Cap (ready-to-feed)	11
Wysoy (powder)	12
Milupa Milumil (powder)	13
Milupa Aptamil (powder)	14
Milupa Prematil (powder)	15
Another kind of milk (please tick and write in the name)	21

. . . .

IF YOU USE LIQUID COW'S MILK PLEASE SAY IF IT IS ORDINARY (WHOLE) MILK, SEMI-SKIMMED OR SKIMMED.

Please do not write in this column

58-59

END 01

3

---

11. Do you buy your baby's milk from the child health clinic?

Yes always 1
Yes sometimes 2
No 3

12. Have you always used the milk mentioned at question 10 or have you changed milks at all (apart from changing from breast milk)?

Have always used the same milk 1 → Q14
Have used other milks 2 → Q13

13. Why did you change brands of milk?

PLEASE TICK ONE OR MORE BOXES

Baby was not satisfied/still hungry 1
Baby kept being sick 2
Baby was constipated 3
Baby was allergic to the milk 4
Other reason (please write in) 5
. . . .

14. At the moment, do you think your baby is more hungry at any particular time of the day than at other times?

Yes 1 → Q15
No 2 → Q16
Don't know 3

Please do not write in this column

START 02

12

13

MC = 3

14
15
16

17

4

15. What time of day is your baby more hungry?

PLEASE TICK ONE OR MORE BOXES

- 6.00 am to before 12.00 noon [1]
- 12.00 noon to before 6.00pm [2]
- 6.00 pm to before midnight [3]
- midnight to before 6.00 am [4]

Please do not write in this column

MC=3
18
19
20

16. Do you get milk tokens for free milk?

Yes [1]
No [2]

21

17. Has your baby ever had any foods such as cereal, rusk or any other kind of solid food?

Yes [1] → (a) - (c)
No [2] → Q21

22

(a) How old was your baby when he/she first had any food apart from milk?

PLEASE ENTER A NUMBER IN THE BOX

[ ] weeks old

23-24

(b) What was the first food your baby had, apart from milk?

PLEASE DESCRIBE FULLY

TYPE OF FOOD ....

BRAND (or say if home made) ....

25-26

5

(c) At which meal did you first offer your baby solid foods?

- Breakfast [1]
- Lunchtime [2]
- Evening meal [3]
- Some other meal (please tick box and write in) [4]
....
- Can't remember/don't know [5]

Please do not write in this column

27

18. At present, are you regularly giving your baby cereal, rusks or any other solid food?

Yes [1] → Q19
No [2] → Q21

28

19. Can you list all the cereal, rusks or solid food that your baby ate yesterday. Please describe each fully, giving the brand name and the stage (1 or 2) if relevant.

Didn't have solids yesterday [1] → Q20

29

TYPE OF FOOD (AND STAGE)	BRAND (OR HOME MADE)

MC = 6
30-31
32-33
34-35
36-37
38-39
40-41

6

20. At which meals do you regularly offer your baby solid food at the moment?

PLEASE TICK ONE OR MORE BOXES

MC = 4

Breakfast [1]

Lunchtime [2]   42

Evening meal [3]   43

Some other meal (please tick box and write in) [4]   44

. . . .   45

21. Apart from milk, do you give your baby water or anything else to drink at the moment?

Yes [1] → (a)

No [2] → Q23

46

(a) Please tick the box if your baby has plain water or write in the drink your baby usually has. Please give the brand name, flavour and say if it is a special baby drink or not.

Plain water [1]

47

BRAND NAME	FLAVOUR	PLEASE TICK IF IT IS A BABY DRINK	
			MC = 3
			48-49
			50-51
			52-53

END 02

7

START 03

22. Do you give your baby drinks mainly . . . . .

PLEASE TICK ONE OR MORE BOXES

MC = 4

Because he/she is thirsty [1]

to give him/her extra vitamins [2]   12

to help his/her colic/wind [3]   13

to help his/her constipation [4]   14

or for some other reason (please tick and write in) [5]   15

23. Do you give your baby any extra vitamins (apart from vitamin drinks mentioned at question 21)?

Yes [1] → (a) & (b)

No [2] → Q24

16

(a) Do you use Children's Vitamin Drops from the child health clinic or another brand?

Children's Vitamin Drops [1]

Other brand (please tick and write in full name) [2]

. . . .

17

(b) How do you usually get the vitamins?

Buy the vitamins myself at the child health clinic [1]

Buy the vitamins somewhere else [2]

Get the vitamins free at the child health clinic [3]

Get vitamins on prescription [4]

Other (please tick and describe) [5]

. . . .

18

8

24. Are you taking any extra vitamins yourself either in tablet or powder form?

Yes [1] →(a)

No [2] →Q25

(a) How do you usually get the vitamins?

Buy the vitamins myself at the child health clinic [1]

Buy the vitamins somewhere else [2]

Get the vitamins free at the child health clinic [3]

Get vitamins on prescription [4]

Other (please tick and describe) [5] . . . .

25. Do you feed your baby on demand or do you generally keep to set feeding times?

On demand [1]

Generally keep to set times [2]

It depends on the circumstances [3]

Please do not write in this column
19
20
21

26. During the last 7 days has your baby woken up during the night between midnight and 6.00 am?

Yes [1] →(a) & (b)

No [2] →Q27

(a) Do you (or your husband/partner) usually feed your baby when he/she wakes up during the night?

Yes [1]

No [2]

(b) For how long has your baby been waking up during the night?

Only started during the last week [1]

For the last two weeks [2]

For the last four weeks [3]

For the last six weeks [4]

Ever since my baby was born [5]

Please do not write in this column
22
23
24

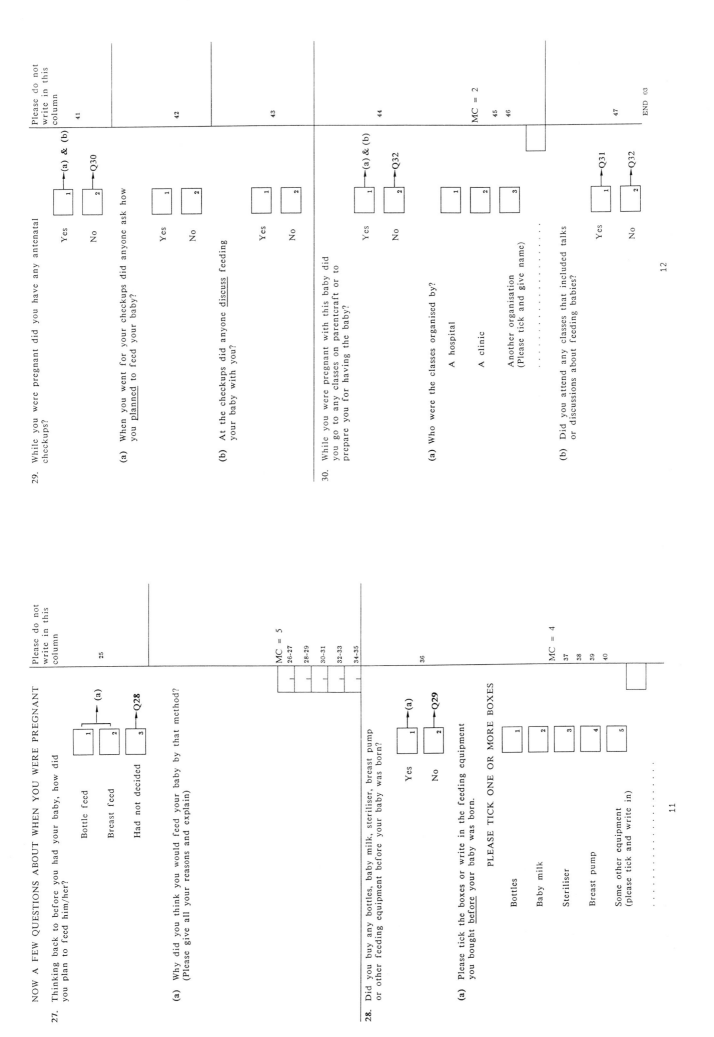

NOW A FEW QUESTIONS ABOUT WHEN YOU WERE PREGNANT

27. Thinking back to before you had your baby, how did you plan to feed him/her?

Bottle feed [1]
Breast feed [2] ── (a)
Had not decided [3] ── Q28

(a) Why did you think you would feed your baby by that method? (Please give all your reasons and explain)

Please do not write in this column

25

MC = 5
26-27
28-29
30-31
32-33
34-35

28. Did you buy any bottles, baby milk, steriliser, breast pump or other feeding equipment before your baby was born?

Yes [1] ── (a)
No [2] ── Q29

(a) Please tick the boxes or write in the feeding equipment you bought before your baby was born.

PLEASE TICK ONE OR MORE BOXES

Bottles [1]
Baby milk [2]
Steriliser [3]
Breast pump [4]
Some other equipment (please tick and write in) [5]
. . . .

36

MC = 4
37
38
39
40

11

29. While you were pregnant did you have any antenatal checkups?

Yes [1] ── (a) & (b)
No [2] ── Q30

(a) When you went for your checkups did anyone ask how you planned to feed your baby?

Yes [1]
No [2]

(b) At the checkups did anyone discuss feeding your baby with you?

Yes [1]
No [2]

Please do not write in this column

41

42

43

30. While you were pregnant with this baby did you go to any classes on parentcraft or to prepare you for having the baby?

Yes [1] ── (a) & (b)
No [2] ── Q32

(a) Who were the classes organised by?

A hospital [1]
A clinic [2]
Another organisation [3]
(Please tick and give name)
. . . .

(b) Did you attend any classes that included talks or discussions about feeding babies?

Yes [1] ── Q31
No [2] ── Q32

44

MC = 2
45
46

47

END 03

12

93

Q31–32

31. (a) Did the classes talk about advantages of breast feeding?

Yes [1]
No [2]

(b) Were you taught how to make up bottles of milk at the classes you attended?

Yes [1]
No [2]

32. When you were pregnant did anyone give you any advice or information about smoking during pregnancy?

Yes [1] → (a)
No [2] → Q33

(a) Who gave you this advice?

PLEASE TICK ONE OR MORE BOXES

Doctor/GP [1]
Health visitor [2]
Midwife/nurse [3]
Friend or relative [4]
Books/leaflets/magazines [5]
Someone else (please tick and write in) [6]

....

Please do not write in this column
START 04
12

13

14

MC = 5
15
16
17
18
19

13

Q33–35

33. When you were pregnant did anyone give you advice or information about drinking alcohol during pregnancy?

Yes [1] → (a)
No [2] → Q34

(a) Who gave you this advice?

PLEASE TICK ONE OR MORE BOXES

Doctor/GP [1]
Health visitor [2]
Midwife/nurse [3]
Friend or relative [4]
Books/leaflets/magazines [5]
Someone else (please tick and write in) [6]

....

34. Did a midwife or health visitor see you at home in connection with your pregnancy before you had the baby?

Yes, midwife [1]
Yes, health visitor [2]
No, neither [3]

35. Do you know any mothers with young babies?

Yes [1] → (a)
No [2] → Q36

(a) Would you say that most of the mothers with young babies you know bottle fed or breast fed?

PLEASE TICK ONE BOX ONLY

Most of them bottle fed [1]
Most of them breast fed [2]
About half of them bottle fed and half of them breast fed [3]
Don't know [4]

Please do not write in this column
20

MC = 5
21
22
23
24
25

MC = 2
26
27

28

29

14

36. Do you know whether you yourself were breast fed when you were a baby?

Breast fed entirely [1]

Bottle fed entirely [2]

Both breast and bottle fed [3]

Don't know [4]

30

NOW A FEW QUESTIONS ABOUT THE BIRTH OF YOUR BABY

37. Was your baby born at home or in hospital?

At home [1] →Q38

In hospital [2] →(a)

31

(a) How long after the baby was born did you stay in hospital?

PLEASE ENTER NUMBER IN ONE BOX ONLY

hours [ ]   OR   days [ ]

32-33   34-35

38. Thinking now of the birth itself, what type of delivery did you have?

Normal [1]

Forceps [2]

Vacuum extraction [3]

Caesarean [4]

36

39. While you were in labour were you given any of these:

PLEASE TICK ONE OR MORE BOXES

MC = 5

An epidural (spinal) injection [1]   37

Another type of injection to lessen the pain (eg pethedine) [2]   38

Gas and oxygen to breathe [3]   39

A general anaesthetic (to make you unconscious) [4]   40

Something else (please tick and write in) [5]   41

. . . .

Nothing at all [6]

END 04

40. How much did your baby weigh when he/she was born?

PLEASE ENTER NUMBERS IN THE BOXES

EITHER [ ] lbs and [ ] OZS

OR [ ] gms

Please do not write in this column
START 05   12-13   14-15
16-19
20-23
24-27

41. (a) What time was your baby born?

PLEASE ENTER TIME IN APPROPRIATE BOX

EITHER [ ] am

OR [ ] pm

(b) About how long after your baby was born did you first hold him/her?

Immediately within a few minutes [1]

Within an hour [2]

More than 1 hour, up to 12 hours [3]

More than 12 hours later [4]

28

42. After the birth were you alright or was anything the matter with you?

Alright [1] → Q43

Something the matter [2] → (a)

29

(a) Did this problem affect your ability to feed your baby the way you wanted to?

Yes [1]

No [2]

30

17

---

43. Was your baby put into special care at all, or put under a lamp for jaundice?

PLEASE TICK ONE OR MORE BOXES

Yes, put into special care [1] ┐ (a)

Yes, put under a lamp [2] ┘

No, neither [3] → Q44

Please do not write in this column
MC = 2
31
32

(a) For how long was your baby put into special care or put under a lamp?

One day or less [1]

Two or three days [2]

Four days or more [3]

33

44. The first time you fed your baby did anyone give you any advice or show you what to do?

Yes [1] → (a) & (b)

No [2] → (c)

34

(a) Who was this?

PLEASE TICK ONE OR MORE BOXES

Nurse/midwife [1]

Doctor [2] → (b)

Someone else (please tick and write in) [3]

. . . .

MC = 3
35
36
37

(b) Was the advice helpful?

Yes [1] → Q45

No [2]

38

(c) Would you have liked any help or advice?

Yes [1]

No [2]

39

18

IF YOU EVER BREAST FED YOUR BABY PLEASE ANSWER QUESTION 45

IF YOUR BABY WAS COMPLETELY BOTTLE FED FROM BIRTH GO ON TO QUESTION 47

45. How soon after your baby was born did you first put him/her to the breast?

Immediately/within a few minutes	[1]
Within half an hour	[2]
More than ½ hr, up to 1 hr later	[3]
More than 1 hr, up to 4 hr later	[4]
More than 4 hr, up to 8 hr later	[5]
More than 8 hr, up to 12 hr later	[6]
More than 12 hr, up to 24 hr later	[7]
More than 24 hr later	[8]

Please do not write in this column

40

IF YOUR BABY WAS BORN IN HOSPITAL PLEASE ANSWER QUESTION 46 OTHERWISE PLEASE GO TO QUESTION 55

46. While you were in hospital did your baby have a bottle of milk (apart from expressed breast milk) as well as being breast fed?

Yes	[1] → (a)
No	[2] → Q48
Do not know	[3]

41

(a) How often did your baby have a bottle in hospital (while you were breast feeding as well)?

Once or twice only	[1]
At every feed	[2] → Q48
Just during the night	[3]
Some other arrangement (please tick and describe)	[4]
....	
Do not know	[5]

42

19

IF YOUR BABY WAS COMPLETELY BOTTLE FED FROM BIRTH PLEASE ANSWER QUESTION 47

47. How soon after he/she was born did you first feed your baby?

Immediately/within a few minutes	[1]
Within half an hour	[2]
More than ½ hr, up to 1 hr later	[3]
More than 1 hr, up to 4 hr later	[4]
More than 4 hr, up to 8 hr later	[5]
More than 8 hr, up to 12 hr later	[6]
More than 12 hr, up to 24 hr later	[7]
More than 24 hr later	[8]

Please do not write in this column

43

20

NOW SOME QUESTIONS ABOUT WHEN YOU WERE IN HOSPITAL

IF YOUR BABY WAS BORN AT HOME PLEASE GO TO QUESTION 55

Please do not write in this column

48. Did your baby stay beside you all the time you were in hospital?

Yes [1] → Q49
No [2] → (a)

44

(a) Even though he/she was not always beside you, did you always feed your baby yourself or did the nurses ever feed him/her?

Always fed baby myself [1] → Q49
Nurses sometimes fed baby [2] → (b)

45

(b) What did the nurses give your baby?

PLEASE TICK ONE OR MORE BOXES

MC = 3

Expressed breast milk [1]
Other baby milk [2]
Dextrose or glucose [3]
Water [4]
Do not know [5]

46
47
48

49. While you were in hospital did you feed your baby on demand or did you keep to set feeding times?

On demand [1]
Set times [2]
Some other arrangement (please tick and describe) [3]
. . . .

49

END 05

Please do not write in this column
START 06

12

50. Were there any problems feeding your baby while you were in hospital?

Yes [1] → (a)
No [2] → Q52

(a) What problems were there? (Please describe)

13-14
15-16
17-18

MC = 3

51. Did anyone give you any help or advice about this/these problems?

Yes [1] → (a)
No [2] → Q52

19

(a) Who helped or advised you?

PLEASE TICK ONE OR MORE BOXES

MC = 3

Midwife [1]
Nurse [2]
Doctor [3]
Someone else (please tick and write in) [4]
. . . .

20
21
22

52. While you were in hospital were you always able to get help or advice when you needed it?

Yes - always [1]
Yes - generally [2]
No [3]

23

53. When you left hospital, were you . . . .

breast feeding completely [1]

bottle feeding completely [2]

or giving both breast and bottle? [3]

24

54. After you left hospital did a midwife come to visit you?

Yes [1] →(a)

No [2] →Q55

25

(a) How soon after you left hospital did she come?

Same day [1]

Next day [2]

Two or more days later [3]

26

55. After you left hospital, did you feel you knew how to get help with feeding your baby if you needed to?

(If your baby was born at home, please base your answer from when your baby was born).

Yes [1]

No [2]

27

56. Since your baby was born has a health visitor been to see you?

Yes [1] →(a)

No [2] →Q57

28

(a) How old was your baby when the health visitor first came?

[ ] days old

29-30

23

---

57. Has your baby had a development check-up yet?

Yes [1] →Q58

No [2] →Q59

31

58. Where did your baby have the development check-up?

At the child health clinic [1]

At your family doctor's (GP) [2]

Somewhere else (please tick and write in) [3]

. . . .

32

59. Have you got help or received advice from a voluntary organisation which helps new mothers (such as the National Childbirth Trust, La Leche League or the Association of Breast Feeding Mothers)?

Yes [1]

No [2]

33

60. Since you left hospital have you had any problems with feeding your baby?

(If your baby was born at home please answer about any feeding problems since the birth)

Yes [1] →(a)

No [2] →Q62

34

(a) What problems have you had? (Please describe)

MC = 4

35-36
37-38
39-40
41-42

24

Page 25

61. Did anyone give you any help or advice about this/these problems?

Yes 1 → (a)

No 2 → Q62

(a) Who helped or advised you?

PLEASE TICK ONE OR MORE BOXES

Midwife or nurse 1

Health visitor 2

Family doctor (GP) 3

Doctor at the child health clinic 4

Friend or relative 5

Someone else (please tick and write in) 6

MC = 4

44
45
46
47

62. During your pregnancy or since the birth of your baby were you given a copy of any of these books?

PLEASE TICK ONE OR MORE BOXES

The Pregnancy Book (Health Education Authority) 1

The Book of the Child (Scottish Health Education Group) 2

The book called "Birth to Five" (Health Education Authority) 3

MC = 3

48
49
50

END 06

Page 26

IF YOU EVER BREAST FED YOUR BABY PLEASE ANSWER QUESTION 63

IF YOUR BABY WAS COMPLETELY BOTTLE FED FROM BIRTH GO TO QUESTION 64

63. Have you ever used a breast pump?

Yes 1 → (a)

No 2 → Q64

(a) What were your reasons for using a breast pump?

PLEASE TICK ONE OR MORE BOXES

Because of painful breasts 1

Because of engorged breasts 2

To express milk for my baby who was ill 3

So that my baby could have breast milk when I was away 4

Other (please tick and write in) 5

MC = 4

13
14
15
16

64. Have you ever smoked cigarettes?

Yes 1 → (a)

No 2 → Q66

17

(a) Do you smoke at all nowadays?

Yes 1 → Q65

No 2 → (b)

18

(b) Have you smoked at all in the past two years?

Yes 1 → Q65

No 2 → Q66

19

65. (a) About how many cigarettes a day were you smoking just before you became pregnant?

20-21

(b) About how many cigarettes a day were you smoking while you were pregnant?

22-23

(c) About how many cigarettes a day are you smoking now?

24-25

PLEASE WRITE IN NUMBER OF CIGARETTES A DAY
(If none write 0)

IF THE NUMBER SMOKED VARIES PLEASE GIVE AN AVERAGE

Page 27

Please do not write in this column

66. Do you ever drink alcohol nowadays, including drinks you brew or make at home? (PLEASE EXCLUDE LOW OR NON ALCOHOLIC DRINKS)

    Yes [1] → Q68
    No [2] → Q67

26

67. Have you drunk alcohol at all during the past two years?

    Yes [1] → Q68
    No [2] → Q72

27

68. Thinking back to when you were pregnant please tick the box that best describes how often you usually drank each of the alcoholic drinks listed below.
(PLEASE EXCLUDE LOW OR NON ALCOHOLIC DRINKS)

During pregnancy I usually drank:

	Most days	3-4 times a week	Once or twice a week	Once or twice a month	Very occas-ionally	Not at all	
Shandy	1	2	3	4	5	6	28
Beer/lager/cider	1	2	3	4	5	6	29
Wine/babycham/champagne	1	2	3	4	5	6	30
Sherry/martini/vermouth/port	1	2	3	4	5	6	31
Spirits/liqueurs	1	2	3	4	5	6	32
Others	1	2	3	4	5	6	33
....	1	2	3	4	5	6	34
....	1	2	3	4	5	6	35

ENTER NAME ON DOTTED LINE & TICK HOW OFTEN

27

Page 28

Please do not write in this column

69. For each type of drink you usually had when you were pregnant, please enter on the dotted lines the amount you usually drank in any one day.

(IF NONE WRITE 0)

Shandy   ..... half pints   36-37

Beer/lager/cider   ..... half pints   38-39

Wine/babycham/champagne   ..... glasses   40-41

Sherry/martini/vermouth/port   ..... glasses   42-43

Spirits/liqueurs   ..... single measures (count double measures as 2)   44-45

Others (please write in name of drink and amount)

....
(name)   (amount)

....
(name)   (amount)

....
(name)   (amount)

28

70. During your pregnancy would you say you drank more, less or about the same amount of alcohol than before you were pregnant?

I drank much more during pregnancy than before   1 → (a)

I drank more during pregnancy than before   2

I drank about the same during pregnancy as before   3 → Q71

I drank less during pregnancy than before   4

I drank much less during pregnancy than before   5 → (a)

46

(a) Why did you change your drinking habits during pregnancy?

PLEASE TICK ONE OR MORE BOXES

Drinking alcohol made me feel sick   01

I disliked the taste of alcohol when I was pregnant   02

Alcohol cheered me up and made me feel better   03

Alcohol might harm my baby   04

I had personal/family problems   05

Some other reason (please tick and write in)   06

MC = 4
47-48
49-50
51-52
53-54

END 07

---

71. Compared with when you were pregnant, would you say you drink more, less or about the same nowadays?

I drink much more nowadays   1 → (a)

I drink more nowadays   2

I drink about the same nowadays   3 → Q72

I drink less nowadays   4

I drink much less nowadays   5 → (a)

(a) Why have you changed your drinking habits since the birth of your baby?

PLEASE TICK ONE OR MORE BOXES

I've had my baby now so I don't have to worry about the effect of alcohol on the baby   01

I've got to like the taste of alcohol again   02

Alcohol cheers me up and makes me feel better   03

Alcohol does not make me feel sick any more   04

Alcohol might affect my milk   05

I do not like the taste of alcohol any more   06

I have personal/family problems   07

Some other reason (please tick and write in)   08

MC = 4
13-14
15-16
17-18
19-20

Page 32

73. Did you ever feel you were being pressurised into breast feeding or bottle feeding this baby?

		Please do not write in this column
Felt pressurised to breast feed	[1]	START 09
Felt pressurised to bottle feed	[2]	12
Did not feel pressurised to breast or bottle feed	[3]	

IF YOUR BABY WAS ENTIRELY BOTTLE FED FROM BIRTH PLEASE GO TO QUESTION 76

IF YOU HAVE EVER BREAST FED YOUR BABY, PLEASE ANSWER QUESTION 74

74. If you had another baby would you breast feed again?

Yes [1]   13
No [2]

IF YOU ARE NOW COMPLETELY BOTTLE FEEDING YOUR BABY GO TO QUESTION 76

IF YOU ARE BREAST FEEDING YOUR BABY ANSWER Q75

75. For how long do you think you will continue breast feeding your baby?

UNTIL MY BABY IS:

PLEASE ENTER NUMBERS IN THE BOXES.

EITHER [ ] weeks old   14-15

OR [ ] months and [ ] weeks old   16-17   18

Don't know/have not decided (please tick if appropriate) [99]   19-20

32

Page 31

IF THIS IS YOUR FIRST BABY PLEASE GO ON TO QUESTION 73

72. If this is not your first baby we would like to know how you fed your previous children. Please fill in the details below, but do not include your latest baby.

PREVIOUS CHILDREN	was he/she breast fed at all?	If breast fed, how long did you continue breast feeding?	Please do not write in this column
FIRST CHILD	Yes [1] / No [2]	[ ] OR days / [ ] OR weeks / [ ] months	21 / 22-23 / 24-25 / 26-27
SECOND CHILD	Yes [1] / No [2]	[ ] OR days / [ ] OR weeks / [ ] months	28 / 29-30 / 31-32 / 33-34
THIRD CHILD	Yes [1] / No [2]	[ ] OR days / [ ] OR weeks / [ ] months	35 / 36-37 / 38-39 / 40-41
FOURTH CHILD	Yes [1] / No [2]	[ ] OR days / [ ] OR weeks / [ ] months	42 / 43-44 / 45-46 / 47-48
FIFTH CHILD	Yes [1] / No [2]	[ ] OR days / [ ] OR weeks / [ ] months	49 / 50-51 / 52-53 / 54-55
SIXTH CHILD	Yes [1] / No [2]	[ ] OR days / [ ] OR weeks / [ ] months	56 / 57-58 / 59-60 / 61-62

END 08

31

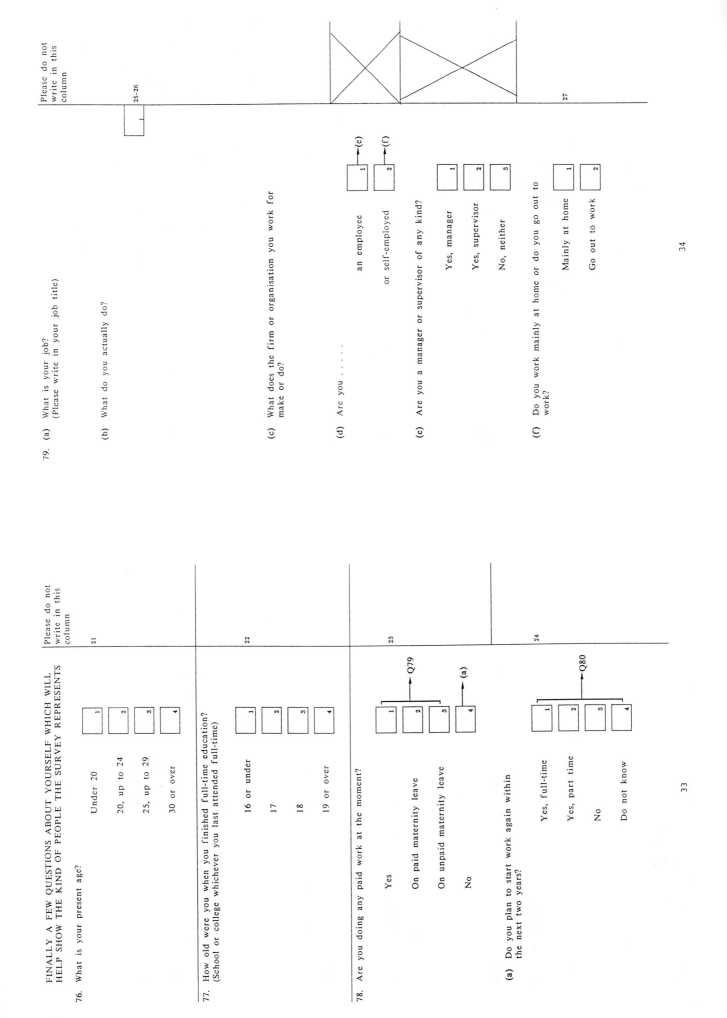

104

FINALLY A FEW QUESTIONS ABOUT YOURSELF WHICH WILL HELP SHOW THE KIND OF PEOPLE THE SURVEY REPRESENTS

76. What is your present age?

Under 20 [1]

20, up to 24 [2]

25, up to 29 [3]

30 or over [4]

77. How old were you when you finished full-time education? (School or college whichever you last attended full-time)

16 or under [1]

17 [2]

18 [3]

19 or over [4]

78. Are you doing any paid work at the moment?

Yes

On paid maternity leave [1]

On unpaid maternity leave [2] → Q79

No [3]

[4] → (a)

(a) Do you plan to start work again within the next two years?

Yes, full-time [1]

Yes, part time [2] → Q80

No [3]

Do not know [4]

33

79. (a) What is your job? (Please write in your job title)

(b) What do you actually do?

(c) What does the firm or organisation you work for make or do?

(d) Are you ......

an employee [1] → (c)

or self-employed [2] → (f)

(e) Are you a manager or supervisor of any kind?

Yes, manager [1]

Yes, supervisor [2]

No, neither [3]

(f) Do you work mainly at home or do you go out to work?

Mainly at home [1]

Go out to work [2]

34

Please do not write in this column

21

22

23

24

25-26

27

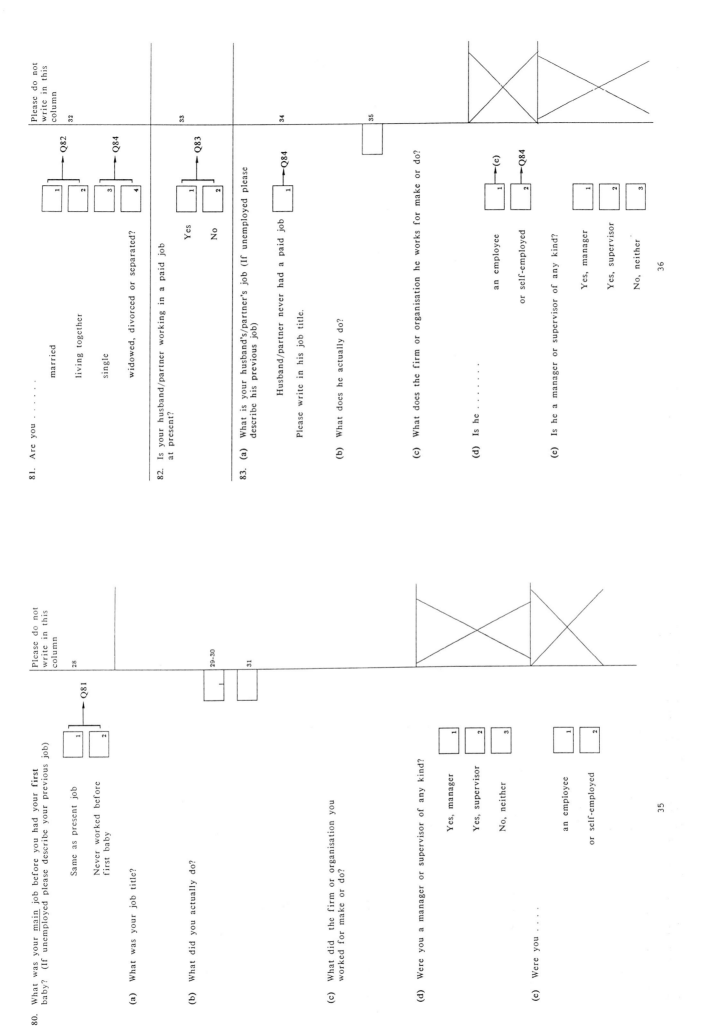

80. What was your **main** job before you had your **first** baby? (If unemployed please describe your previous job)

Same as present job — [1] → Q81
Never worked before first baby — [2]

28

(a) What was your job title?

29-30

(b) What did you actually do?

31

(c) What did the firm or organisation you worked for make or do?

(d) Were you a manager or supervisor of any kind?

Yes, manager [1]
Yes, supervisor [2]
No, neither [3]

(e) Were you . . . .

an employee [1]
or self-employed [2]

35

---

81. Are you . . . . . .

married [1] → Q82
living together [2]
single [3] → Q84
widowed, divorced or separated? [4]

32

82. Is your husband/partner working in a paid job at present?

Yes [1] → Q83
No [2]

33

83. (a) What is your husband's/partner's job? (If unemployed please describe his previous job)

Husband/partner never had a paid job [1] → Q84

Please write in his job title.

34

(b) What does he actually do?

35

(c) What does the firm or organisation he works for make or do?

(d) Is he . . . .

an employee [1] → (e)
or self-employed [2] → Q84

(e) Is he a manager or supervisor of any kind?

Yes, manager [1]
Yes, supervisor [2]
No, neither [3]

36

105

84. Is there anything else you would like to say about feeding your baby?

Yes [1] ──▸ please write in below

No [2]

Please give the date when you filled in this questionnaire

day [ ]   month [ ]   year [19]

WAS THERE ANYTHING YOU INTENDED TO GO BACK AND COMPLETE?   PLEASE CHECK.

Thank you very much for your help.

We hope to contact mothers again later to see how they are feeding their babies when they are a little older. If you expect to move house in the near future and know your new address it would help us if you could write it below:

Stage 2 questionnaire

┌─────────────────────────┐
│ OFFICE USE ONLY   │
│ N1299/21   │
│   │
│ STAGE ¹⁴   [2]   │
│ BREAST ¹⁵ = 1   [ ]   │
│ BOTTLE = 2   [ ]   │
│ OUTCOME ¹⁶/¹⁷   [ ]   │
└─────────────────────────┘

SURVEY OF INFANT FEEDING

1. Most questions on the following pages can be answered simply by putting a tick in the box next to the answer that applies to you

   Example:

   Yes [✓] 1

   No [ ] 2

   Sometimes you are asked to write in a number or the answer in your own words. Please enter numbers as figures rather than words.

2. Occasionally you may have more than 1 answer to a question. Please tick all the boxes next to the answers that apply to you if the instruction **"PLEASE TICK ONE OR MORE BOXES"** is printed on top of the boxes.

3. Usually after answering each question you go on to the next one unless a box you have ticked has an arrow next to it with an instruction to go to another question

   Example:

   Yes [✓] 1 → Q5

   No [ ] 2

   By following the arrows carefully you will miss out some questions which do not apply to you, so the amount you have to fill in will make the questionnaire shorter than it looks.

4. If you cannot remember, do not know, or are unable to answer a particular question please write that in.

5. If, rather than a single baby, you have twins or triplets, please answer the questions in relation to the one who was born first.

6. When you have finished please post the questionnaire to us as soon as possible in the reply-paid envelope provided, even if you were not able to answer all of it.

   The names and addresses of people who co-operate in surveys are held in strict confidence by OPCS and never passed to any other Government Department, or to members of the public or press.

   We shall be very grateful for your help

   ┌──┐
   │ If for any reason your baby is no longer with you please tick the box below and return the questionnaire to us so we do not trouble you further. │
   │   │
   │ My baby is no longer with me   [ ]   │
   └──┘

FIRST OF ALL WE WOULD LIKE TO ASK SOME GENERAL QUESTIONS BEFORE FINDING OUT HOW YOU FEED YOUR BABY AT PRESENT.

	Please do not write in this column

1 May I just check, what is your baby's first or Christian name?
(Please write in below 1 letter per box)

2 How old is your baby?

PLEASE ENTER NUMBERS IN BOTH BOXES

weeks   days

and

18 - 32

33 - 34   35

3 Are you still breast feeding your baby at all?

Yes [1] → (a) - (c)

No [2] → Q4

36

(a) Do you breast feed your baby on demand or do you generally keep to set feeding times?

On demand [1]

Generally keep to set times [2]

It depends on the circumstances [3]

37

(b) How often do you breast feed your baby now?

Once a day [1]

Twice a day [2]

3 - 4 times a day [3]

5 - 6 times a day [4]

7 - 8 times a day [5]

More than 8 times a day [6]

(Please tick and write in number of times)

....

38

(c) Do you give your baby milk from a bottle at present (apart from expressed breast milk)?

Yes [1] → Q6

No [2] → Q9

39

1

4 How old was your baby when you last breast fed him/her?

PLEASE ENTER NUMBERS IN BOTH BOXES

weeks   days

and

40 - 41   42

(a) What were your reasons for stopping breast feeding?
(Please explain all your reasons)

MC = 5

43 - 44
45 - 46
47 - 48
49 - 50
51 - 52

5 Would you like to have continued breast feeding for longer (or had you breast fed for as long as you intended)?

Would have liked to have breast fed longer [1]

I have breast fed for as long as intended [2]

53

2

Right column (questions 7-10)

	Please do not write in this column

7. How old was your baby when you started giving this kind of milk?

PLEASE ENTER A NUMBER IN THE BOX

[ ] weeks old   56 - 57

8. Do you buy your baby's milk from the child health clinic?

Yes always [1]
Yes sometimes [2]
No [3]   58

9. Do you get milk tokens for free milk?

Yes [1]
No [2]   59

10. At the moment do you think your baby is more hungry at any particular time of the day than at other times?

Yes [1] → Q11
No [2] ┐
Don't know [3] ┘ → Q12   60

END 01

4

Left column (question 6, page 3)

	Please do not write in this column
	54 - 55

6. Which kind of milk do you give your baby most of the time at the moment?

PLEASE TICK ONE BOX ONLY

Cow and Gate Premium (powder) [01]
Cow and Gate Premium (ready-to-feed) [02]
Cow and Gate Plus (powder) [03]
Cow and Gate Plus (ready-to-feed) [04]
Cow and Gate Formula S (powder) [05]
Ostermilk Two (powder) [06]
Ostersoy (powder) [07]
SMA Gold Cap (powder) [08]
SMA Gold Cap (ready-to-feed) [09]
SMA White Cap (powder) [10]
SMA White Cap (ready-to-feed) [11]
Wysoy (powder) [12]
Milupa Milumil (powder) [13]
Milupa Aptamil (powder) [14]
Milupa Prematil (powder) [15]
Progress (powder) [16]
Farley's Junior Milk (powder) [17]
Boots Junior Milk (powder) [22]
Liquid cow's milk - whole [18]
- semi-skimmed [19]
- skimmed [20]

Another kind of milk
(please tick and write in the name) [21]
....

3

Page 5

11. What time of day is your baby more hungry?

PLEASE TICK ONE OR MORE BOXES

6.00 am to before 12.00 noon	[1]	12
12.00 noon to before 6.00 pm	[2]	13
6.00 pm to before midnight	[3]	14
midnight to before 6.00am	[4]	

NOW A FEW QUESTIONS ON SOLID FOODS

12. Do you give your baby foods such as cereal, rusks or any other kind of solid food including any that you make yourself?

Yes [1] → (a)
No [2] → Q19

15

(a) How old was your baby when he/she first had any food apart from milk?

PLEASE ENTER A NUMBER IN THE BOX

[ ] weeks old

16 - 17

13. At which meal did you first offer your baby solid foods?

Breakfast [1]
Lunchtime [2]
Evening meal [3]
Some other meal (please tick box and write in) [4] ....
Can't remember/don't know [5]

18

Page 6

19

14. Can you list all the cereal, rusks or solid food your baby ate yesterday. Please describe each fully, giving the brand name or if its home made, whether commercial baby food is dried or tinned/jarred and also the time of the feed.

Didn't have solids yesterday [1] → Q15

Time of feed	Type of food	Brand (or home made)	Please tick to show whether dried / tinned/jarred	
				20 - 21
				22 - 23
				24 - 25
				26 - 27
				28 - 29
				30 - 31
				32 - 33

15. Do you use milk to mix up your baby's food?

Yes [1] → (a)
No [2] → Q16

34

(a) Do you use

infant formula milk [1]
or liquid cow's milk [2]
or something else (please tick and write in) [3] ....

35

16. At which meals do you regularly offer your baby solid food at the moment?

PLEASE TICK ONE OR MORE BOXES

Breakfast [1] 36
Lunchtime [2] 37
Evening meal [3] 38
Some other meal (please tick box and write in) [4] 39 ....

Page 7

IF YOUR BABY USUALLY HAS THREE MEALS OF SOLID FOODS A DAY PLEASE ANSWER QUESTION 17. OTHERWISE PLEASE GO TO QUESTION 18.

Please do not write in this column

17. How old was your baby when he/she regularly started having three meals of solid foods a day?

PLEASE ENTER A NUMBER IN THE BOX

[ ] weeks old   40 - 41

18. What do you take into account when deciding what solid foods to give your baby?

MC = 5
42 - 43
44 - 45
46 - 47
48 - 49
50 - 51

19. Apart from milk, do you give your baby water or anything else to drink at the moment?

Yes [1] → (a)
No [2] → Q22
52

(a) Do you give your baby bottled mineral water at all?

Yes [1] → (b)
No [2] → Q20
53

(b) When you give your baby mineral water do you use mineral water bottled especially for babies?

Yes, always [1]
Yes, sometimes [2]
No, never [3]
54

END 02

7

Page 8

Please do not write in this column

START 03

20. Apart from mineral water, what other drinks do you give your baby? Please tick the box if your baby has tap water or write in the drink your baby usually has. Please give the brand name, flavour and say if it is a special baby drink or not.

Tap water [1]   12

BRAND NAME	FLAVOUR	PLEASE TICK IF IT IS A BABY DRINK	
			MC = 5 13 - 14
			15 - 16
			17 - 18
			19 - 20
			21 - 22

21. Do you give your baby drinks mainly . . . .

PLEASE TICK ONE OR MORE BOXES

because your baby is thirsty [1]

to give your baby extra vitamins [2]

to help your baby's digestion [3]

or for some other reason (please tick and write in) [4]
. . . .

MC = 4
23
24
25
26

8

22. Do you give your baby any extra vitamins (apart from vitamin drinks mentioned at question 20)?

Yes [1] → (a) & (b)

No [2] → Q23

[27]

(a) Do you use Children's Vitamin Drops from the child health clinic or another brand?

Children's Vitamin Drops [1]

Other brand (please tick and write in full name) [2]

. . . .

[28]

(b) How do you usually get the vitamins?

Buy the vitamins myself at the child health clinic [1]

Buy the vitamins somewhere else [2]

Get the vitamins free at the child health clinic [3]

Get vitamins on prescription [4]

Other (please tick and describe) [5]

. . . .

[29]

9

---

23. Are you taking any extra vitamins yourself either in tablet or powder form?

Yes [1] → (a)

No [2] → Q24

[30]

(a) How do you usually get the vitamins?

Buy the vitamins myself at the child health clinic [1]

Buy the vitamins somewhere else [2]

Get the vitamins free at the child health clinic [3]

Get vitamins on prescription [4]

Other (please tick and describe) [5]

. . . .

[31]

24. During the last 7 days has your baby woken up during the night between midnight and 6.00 am?

Yes [1] → (a) & (b)

No [2] → Q25

[32]

(a) Do you (or your husband/partner) usually feed your baby when he/she wakes up during the night?

Yes [1]

No [2]

[33]

(b) For how long has your baby been waking up during the night?

Only started during the last week [1]

For the last two weeks [2]

For the last month [3]

For the last two months [4]

For the last three months [5]

Ever since my baby was born [6]

[34]

10

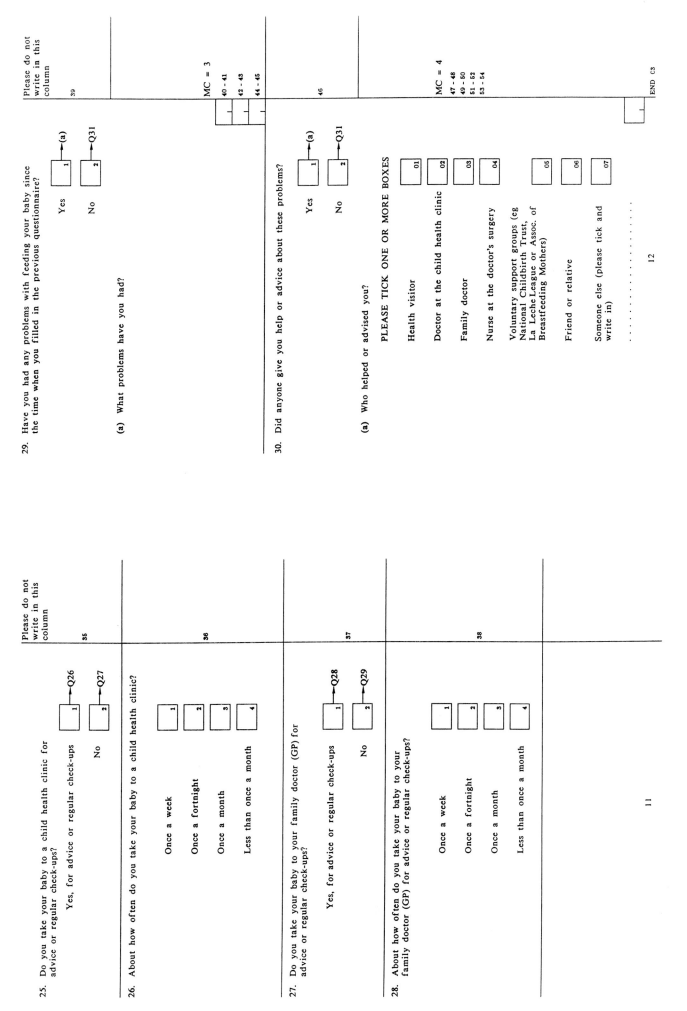

25. Do you take your baby to a child health clinic for advice or regular check-ups?

Yes, for advice or regular check-ups [1] → Q26

No [2] → Q27

26. About how often do you take your baby to a child health clinic?

Once a week [1]

Once a fortnight [2]

Once a month [3]

Less than once a month [4]

27. Do you take your baby to your family doctor (GP) for advice or regular check-ups?

Yes, for advice or regular check-ups [1] → Q28

No [2] → Q29

28. About how often do you take your baby to your family doctor (GP) for advice or regular check-ups?

Once a week [1]

Once a fortnight [2]

Once a month [3]

Less than once a month [4]

29. Have you had any problems with feeding your baby since the time when you filled in the previous questionnaire?

Yes [1] → (a)

No [2] → Q31

(a) What problems have you had?

30. Did anyone give you help or advice about these problems?

Yes [1] → (a)

No [2] → Q31

(a) Who helped or advised you?

PLEASE TICK ONE OR MORE BOXES

Health visitor [01]

Doctor at the child health clinic [02]

Family doctor [03]

Nurse at the doctor's surgery [04]

Voluntary support groups (eg National Childbirth Trust, La Leche League or Assoc. of Breastfeeding Mothers) [05]

Friend or relative [06]

Someone else (please tick and write in) .... [07]

Please do not write in this column

35

36

37

38

39

MC = 3

40 - 41
42 - 43
44 - 45

46

MC = 4

47 - 48
49 - 50
51 - 52
53 - 54

END C3

Page 13

Please do not write in this column

START 04

12

31. Has anyone given you help or advice on breast feeding since the time you filled in the previous questionnaire?

Yes [1] → Q32

No [2] → Q33

Have not ask for help or advice [3]

32. Who helped or advised you on breast feeding?

PLEASE TICK ONE OR MORE BOXES

MC = 4
13 - 14
15 - 16
17 - 18
19 - 20

Health visitor [01]

Doctor at the child health clinic [02]

Family doctor [03]

Nurse at the doctor's surgery [04]

Voluntary support groups (eg National Childbirth Trust, La Leche League or Assoc. of Breastfeeding Mothers) [05]

Friend or relative [06]

Someone else (please tick and write in)
. . . . [07]

21

33. Do you smoke cigarettes at all nowadays?

Yes [1]

No [2]

22

34. Does your husband/partner smoke cigarettes at all nowadays?

Yes [1]

No [2]

13

Page 14

Please do not write in this column

23 - 24

IF YOU SMOKE CIGARETTES NOWADAYS PLEASE ANSWER QUESTION 35 OTHERWISE PLEASE GO TO QUESTION 36.

35. About how many cigarettes a day do you usually smoke now?

PLEASE ENTER NUMBER IN THE BOX [ ]

25 - 26

IF YOUR HUSBAND/PARTNER SMOKES CIGARETTES NOWADAYS PLEASE ANSWER QUESTION 36. OTHERWISE PLEASE GO TO QUESTION 37.

36. About how many cigarettes a day does your husband/partner usually smoke now?

PLEASE ENTER NUMBER IN THE BOX [ ]

27

37. Are you doing any paid work at the moment?

Yes [1]

On paid maternity leave [2] → Q38

On unpaid maternity leave [3]

No [4] → (a)

28

(a) Do you plan to start work again within the next two years?

Yes, full time [1]

Yes, part time [2] → Q40

No [3]

Do not know [4]

14

38. (a) What is your job?
(Please write in your job title)

(b) What do you actually do?

(c) What does the firm or organisation you work for make or do?

(d) Are you ......

    an employee [1]

    or self-employed [2]

(e) Are you a manager or supervisor of any kind?

    Yes, manager [1]

    Yes, supervisor [2]

    No, neither [3]

(f) Do you work mainly at home or do you go out to work?

    Mainly at home [1]

    Go out to work [2]

15

IF YOU ARE WORKING AT THE MOMENT PLEASE ANSWER QUESTION 39. OTHERWISE PLEASE GO TO QUESTION 40.

39. When you are working who usually looks after the baby?

PLEASE TICK **ONE** BOX ONLY

    No-one apart from me [1]

    Husband or partner [2]

    Mother or mother-in-law [3]

    Childminder [4]

    Nursery or creche [5]

    Someone else (please tick and write in) [6] → (a)

    ....

(a) Do you pay to have the baby looked after?

    Yes [1]

    No [2]

40. Some people find it difficult to manage with a young baby when they go out to public places.

Have you ever had problems finding somewhere to feed your baby when you were out in public places?

    Yes [1] →

    No [2] → Q41

    Only go out between feeds [3] → Q43

41. Have you ever breast fed your baby in a public place? (Please exclude hospitals).

    Yes [1] → Q42

    No [2] → Q43

    Bottle fed from birth [3] → Q43

16

115

Please do not write in this column

42. When you breast feed in a public place do you:

prefer a mother and baby room? [1]

prefer to breastfeed without going to any special place? [2]

no preference [3]

36

43. Where do you think that it is important to have facilities for feeding babies?

Shops/shopping centres [1]

Restaurants [2]

Public toilets [3]

Other places (please tick and write in) . . . . [4]

37

44. Is there anything else you would like to say about feeding your baby?

Yes [1] → please write in below

No [2]

38

17

Please give the date when you filled in this questionnaire

day month year

[ ] [ ] 19[ ]

WAS THERE ANYTHING YOU INTENDED TO GO BACK AND COMPLETE? PLEASE CHECK.

Thank you very much for your help.

We hope to contact mothers again later to see how they are feeding their babies when they are a little older. If you expect to move house in the near future and know your new address it would help us if you could write it below:

18

Stage 3 questionnaire

SURVEY OF INFANT FEEDING

1. Most questions on the following pages can be answered simply by putting a tick in the box next to the answer that applies to you

   Example:

   Yes ☑ 1

   No ☐ 2

   Sometimes you are asked to write in a number or the answer in your own words. Please enter numbers as figures rather than words.

2. Occasionally you may have more than 1 answer to a question. Please tick all the boxes next to the answers that apply to you if the instruction "PLEASE TICK ONE OR MORE BOXES" is printed on top of the boxes.

3. Usually after answering each question you go on to the next one unless a box you have ticked has an arrow next to it with an instruction to go to another question

   Example:

   Yes ☑ 1 → Q5

   No ☐ 2

4. By following the arrows carefully you will miss out some questions which do not apply to you, so the amount you have to fill in will make the questionnaire shorter than it looks.

5. If you cannot remember, do not know, or are unable to answer a particular question please write that in.

6. If, rather than a single baby, you have twins or triplets, please answer the questions in relation to the one who was born first.

   When you have finished please post the questionnaire to us as soon as possible in the reply-paid envelope provided, even if you were not able to answer all of it.

   The names and addresses of people who co-operate in surveys are held in strict confidence by OPCS and never passed to any other Government Department, or to members of the public or press.

   We shall be very grateful for your help

If for any reason your baby is no longer with you please tick the box below and return the questionnaire to us so we do not trouble you you further.
My baby is no longer with me ☐

Page 1

FIRST OF ALL WE WOULD LIKE TO ASK SOME GENERAL QUESTIONS BEFORE FINDING OUT HOW YOU FEED YOUR BABY AT PRESENT.

1 What is your baby's first or Christian name?
(Please write in below 1 letter per box)

□□□□□□□□□□□□

2. How old is your baby?　PLEASE ENTER NUMBERS IN BOTH BOXES

weeks □ and □ days　　18 - 32 · 33 - 34 · 35

3. Are you still breast feeding your baby at all?

Yes □ 1 → (a) - (c)
No □ 2 → Q4　　36

(a) Do you breast feed your baby on demand or do you generally keep to set feeding times?

On demand □ 1
Generally keep to set times □ 2
It depends on the circumstances □ 3　　37

(b) How often do you breast feed your baby now?

Once a day □ 1
Twice a day □ 2
3 - 4 times a day □ 3
5 - 6 times a day □ 4
7 - 8 times a day □ 5
More than 8 times a day □ 6

(Please tick and write in number of times)　　38

(c) Do you give your baby milk from a bottle or cup at present (apart from expressed breast milk)?

Yes, from a bottle or cup □ 1 → Q6
No □ 2 → Q9　　39

1

Page 2

4. How old was your baby when you last breast fed him/her?
PLEASE ENTER NUMBERS IN BOTH BOXES

weeks □ and □ days　　40 - 41 · 42

(a) What were your reasons for stopping breast feeding?
(Please explain all your reasons)

MC = 5
□ 43 - 44
□ 45 - 46
□ 47 - 48
□ 49 - 50
□ 51 - 52

5. Would you like to have continued breast feeding for longer or had you breast fed for as long as you intended?

Would have liked to have breast fed longer □ 1
I have breast fed for as long as intended □ 2　　53

2

6. Which kinds of milk do you give your baby to drink at the moment (apart from breast milk)?

	Usual milk	Other milk
Cow and Gate Premium (powder)	01	01
Cow and Gate Premium (ready-to-feed)	02	02
Cow and Gate Plus (powder)	03	03
Cow and Gate Plus (ready-to-feed)	04	04
Cow and Gate Formula S (powder)	05	05
Ostermilk (powder)	23	23
Ostermilk Two (powder)	06	06
Ostersoy (powder)	07	07
SMA Gold Cap (powder)	08	08
SMA Gold Cap (ready-to-feed)	09	09
SMA White Cap (powder)	10	10
SMA White Cap (ready-to-feed)	11	11
Wysoy (powder)	12	12
Milupa Milumil (powder)	13	13
Milupa Aptamil (powder)	14	14
Progress (powder)	16	16
Farley's Junior Milk (powder)	17	17
Boots Junior Milk (powder)	22	22
Liquid cow's milk - whole	18	18
- semi-skimmed	19	19
- skimmed	20	20
Another kind of milk (please tick and write in the name)	21	21

Please do not write in this column

54 - 55
56 - 57

END 01

3

7. How old was your baby when you started giving the milks mentioned in Question 6?

Usual milk — weeks old — Gave from birth 00

Other milk — weeks old — Gave from birth 00

8. Do you buy your baby's milk from the child health clinic?

Yes always 1

Yes sometimes 2

No 3

9. Do you get milk tokens for free milk?

Yes 1

No 2

10. At the moment do you think your baby is more hungry at any particular time of the day than at other times?

Yes 1 → Q11

No 2 → Q12

Don't know 3 → Q12

Please do not write in this column

START C2

12 - 13   14 - 15

16

17

18

4

119

Please do not write in this column

11. What time of day is your baby more hungry?

PLEASE TICK ONE OR MORE BOXES

		MC = 3
6.00 am to before 12.00 noon	[1]	19
12.00 noon to before 6.00 pm	[2]	20
6.00 pm to before midnight	[3]	21
midnight to before 6.00am	[4]	

12. Apart from milk, do you give your baby water or anything else to drink at the moment?

Yes [1] → (a) & (b)
No [2] → Q14.   22

(a) Do you give your baby bottled mineral water at all?

Yes [1] → (b)
No [2] → Q13   23

(b) When you give your baby mineral water do you use mineral water bottled especially for babies?

Yes, always [1]
Yes, sometimes [2]
No, never [3]   24

13. Apart from mineral water, what other drinks do you give your baby? Please tick the box if your baby has tap water or write in the drink your baby usually has. Please give the brand name, flavour and say if it is a special baby drink or not.

Tap water [ ]   25

BRAND NAME	FLAVOUR	PLEASE TICK IF IT IS A BABY DRINK	MC = 5
			26-27
			28-29
			30-31
			32-33
			34-35

5

Please do not write in this column

14. Do you give your baby any extra vitamins (apart from vitamin drinks mentioned at question 13)?

Yes [1] → (a) & (b)
No [2] → Q15   36

(a) Do you use Children's Vitamin Drops from the child health clinic or another brand?

Children's Vitamin Drops [1]
Other brand (please tick and write in full name) [2]
. . . .   37

(b) How do you usually get the vitamins?

Buy the vitamins myself at the child health clinic [1]
Buy the vitamins somewhere else [2]
Get the vitamins free at the child health clinic [3]
Get vitamins on prescription [4]
Other (please tick and describe) [5]
. . . .   38

15. Are you taking any extra vitamins yourself either in tablet or powder form?

Yes [1] → (a)
No [2] → Q16   39

(a) How do you usually get the vitamins?

Buy the vitamins myself at the child health clinic [1]
Buy the vitamins somewhere else [2]
Get the vitamins free at the child health clinic [3]
Get vitamins on prescription [4]
Other (please tick and describe) [5]
. . . .   40

6

NOW A FEW QUESTIONS ON SOLID FOODS

Please do not write in this column

16. Do you give your baby foods such as cereal, rusks or any other kind of solid food including any that you make yourself?

Yes 1 → (a)
No 2 → Q27

41

(a) How old was your baby when he/she first had any food apart from milk?

PLEASE ENTER A NUMBER IN THE BOX

[ ] weeks old

42-43

17. Have you ever used liquid cow's milk for mixing solid foods?

Yes 1 → (a)
No 2 → Q18

44

(a) Hold old was your baby when you first gave him/her liquid cow's milk in this way?

PLEASE ENTER A NUMBER IN THE BOX

[ ] weeks old

45-46

18. At which meal did you first offer your baby solid foods?

Breakfast 1
Lunchtime 2
Evening meal 3
Some other meal (please tick box and write in) 4
. . . .
Can't remember/don't know 5

47

END 02

7

Please do not write in this column

19. Can you list all the cereal, rusks or solid food that your baby ate yesterday. Please describe each fully, giving the brand name or if it's home made, whether the commercial baby food is dried or tinned/jarred and also the time of the meal.

START 03
12

Didn't have solids yesterday 1 → Q20

Time of day	Type of food	Brand (or home made)	Please tick to show whether dried	tinned/jarred	MC = 10
					13-14
					15-16
					17-18
					19-20
					21-22
					23-24
					25-26
					27-28
					29-30
					31-32

20. IF YOU HAVE EVER GIVEN YOUR BABY HOME MADE SOLID FOODS PLEASE ANSWER QUESTION 20. OTHERWISE GO TO QUESTION 21.

When you give your baby home made solid food do you usually:

PLEASE TICK ONE BOX ONLY

sieve, blend or liquidise the food to a puree? 1

mash the food up? 2

mince the food? 3

cut up the food finely? 4

use some other way to make the food suitable for your baby? (please tick and write in) 5
. . . .

33

8

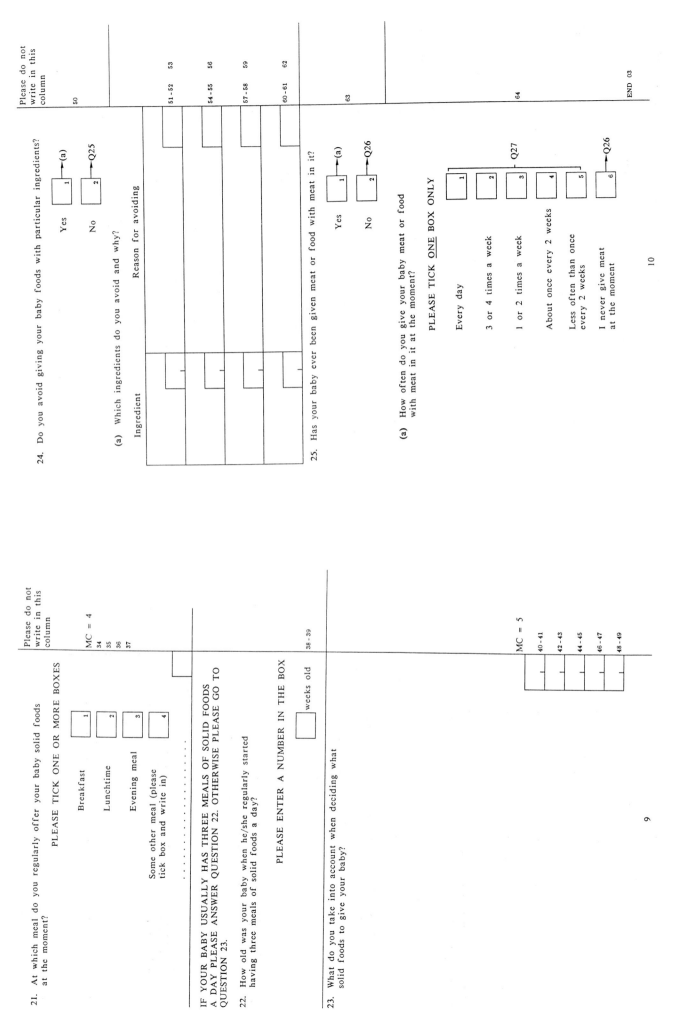

Page 9

21. At which meal do you regularly offer your baby solid foods at the moment?

PLEASE TICK ONE OR MORE BOXES

Breakfast [1]

Lunchtime [2]

Evening meal [3]

Some other meal (please tick box and write in) [4]

....

MC = 4
34
35
36
37

IF YOUR BABY USUALLY HAS THREE MEALS OF SOLID FOODS A DAY PLEASE ANSWER QUESTION 22. OTHERWISE PLEASE GO TO QUESTION 23.

22. How old was your baby when he/she regularly started having three meals of solid foods a day?

PLEASE ENTER A NUMBER IN THE BOX

[ ] weeks old

38-39

23. What do you take into account when deciding what solid foods to give your baby?

MC = 5
40-41
42-43
44-45
46-47
48-49

Page 10

24. Do you avoid giving your baby foods with particular ingredients?

Yes [1] (a)

No [2] Q25

50

(a) Which ingredients do you avoid and why?

Ingredient	Reason for avoiding
		51-52 53
		54-55 56
		57-58 59
		60-61 62

25. Has your baby ever been given meat or food with meat in it?

Yes [1] (a)

No [2] Q26

63

(a) How often do you give your baby meat or food with meat in it at the moment?

PLEASE TICK ONE BOX ONLY

Every day [1]

3 or 4 times a week [2]

1 or 2 times a week [3]   } Q27

About once every 2 weeks [4]

Less often than once every 2 weeks [5]

I never give meat at the moment [6] Q26

64

END 03

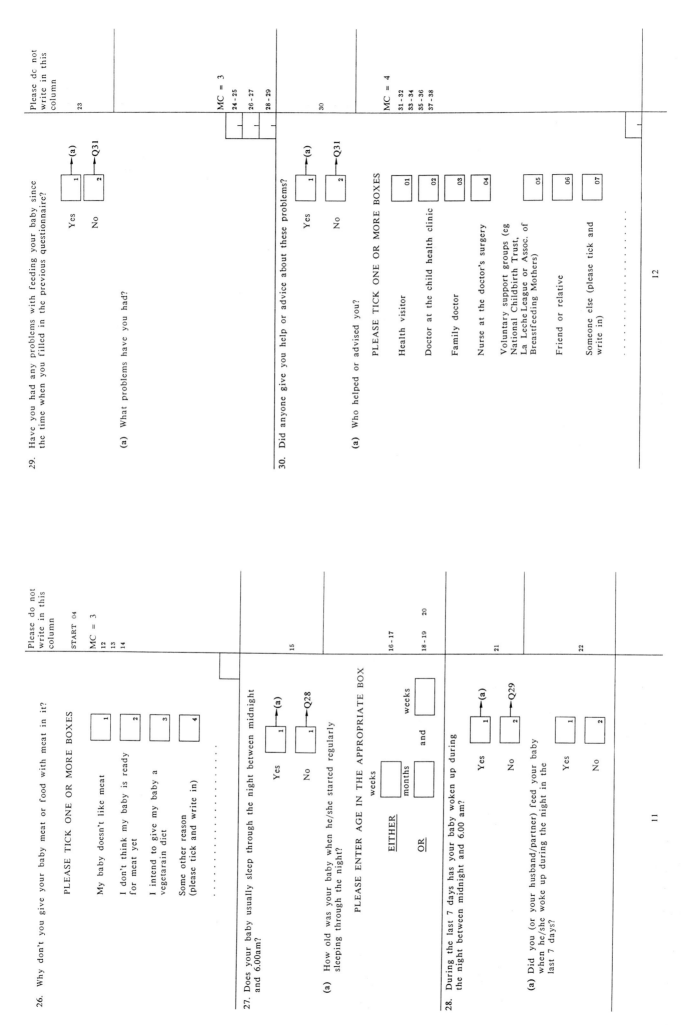

29. Have you had any problems with feeding your baby since the time when you filled in the previous questionnaire?

Yes [1] → (a)

No [2] → Q31

23

(a) What problems have you had?

MC = 3
24-25
26-27
28-29

30. Did anyone give you help or advice about these problems?

Yes [1] → (a)

No [2] → Q31

30

(a) Who helped or advised you?

PLEASE TICK ONE OR MORE BOXES

MC = 4

Health visitor [01]   31-32

Doctor at the child health clinic [02]   33-34

Family doctor [03]   35-36

Nurse at the doctor's surgery [04]   37-38

Voluntary support groups (eg National Childbirth Trust, La Leche League or Assoc. of Breastfeeding Mothers) [05]

Friend or relative [06]

Someone else (please tick and write in) [07]

12

26. Why don't you give your baby meat or food with meat in it?

PLEASE TICK ONE OR MORE BOXES

START 04

MC = 3

My baby doesn't like meat [1]   12

I don't think my baby is ready for meat yet [2]   13

I intend to give my baby a vegetarian diet [3]   14

Some other reason (please tick and write in) [4]

27. Does your baby usually sleep through the night between midnight and 6.00am?

Yes [1] → (a)

No [1] → Q28

15

(a) How old was your baby when he/she started regularly sleeping through the night?

PLEASE ENTER AGE IN THE APPROPRIATE BOX

weeks

EITHER [months]   16-17

OR [ ] and [ ] weeks   18-19   20

28. During the last 7 days has your baby woken up during the night between midnight and 6.00 am?

Yes [1] → (a)

No [2] → Q29

21

(a) Did you (or your husband/partner) feed your baby when he/she woke up during the night in the last 7 days?

Yes [1]

No [2]

22

11

31.

Thinking back since your baby was born who has been the most helpful in giving you general advice on feeding your baby?

PLEASE TICK ONE OR MORE BOXES

Midwife or nurse at the hospital [01]

Health visitor [02]

Family doctor [03]

Doctor at the child health clinic [04]

Nurse at the child health clinic [05]

Voluntary support groups (eg National Childbirth Trust, La Leche League or Assoc. of Breastfeeding Mothers) [06]

Friend or relative [07]

Someone else (please tick and write in) [08]

....

Have not been given any help or advice [09]

Please do not write in this column

MC = 4
39-40
41-42
43-44
45-46

32.

Are you doing any paid work at the moment?

Yes - go out to work [1] → Q33

Yes - work at home [2]

On paid maternity leave [3] → Q34

On unpaid maternity leave [4]

No [5] → (a)

47

(a) Do you plan to start work again within the next two years?

Yes, full time [1]

Yes, part time [2] → Q36

No [3]

Do not know [4]

48

13

FOR MOTHERS WHO ARE STILL BREAST FEEDING. IF YOU ARE NOT BREAST FEEDING PLEASE GO TO QUESTION 34.

33.

How do you usually feed your baby while you are at work?

PLEASE TICK ONE OR MORE BOXES

Take baby with me to work [1]

Express breast milk for baby to have while I am at work [2]

Baby has other milk while I am at work [3]

Other arrangement (please tick and describe) [4]

Please do not write in this column

MC = 3
49
50
51

34.

(a) What is your job? (Please write in your job title)

(b) What do you actually do?

52-53

(c) What does the firm or organisation you work for make or do?

(d) Are you . . . . . .

an employee [1]

or self-employed [2]

(e) Are you a manager or supervisor of any kind?

Yes, manager [1]

Yes, supervisor [2]

No, neither [3]

END 04

14

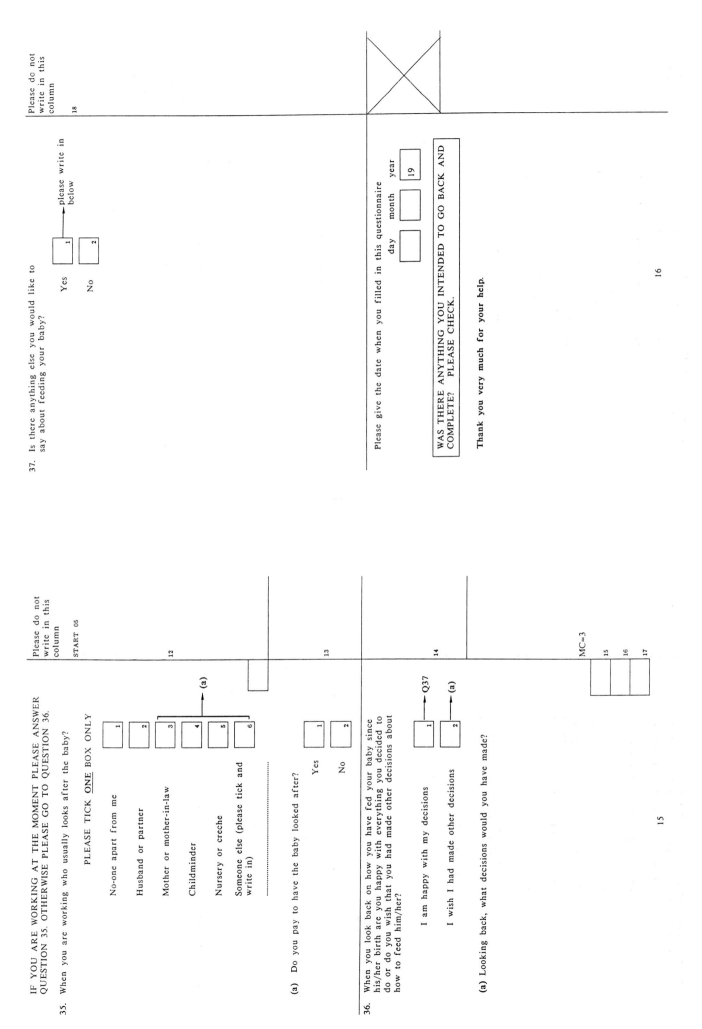

Please do not write in this column

START 05

IF YOU ARE WORKING AT THE MOMENT PLEASE ANSWER QUESTION 35. OTHERWISE PLEASE GO TO QUESTION 36.

35. When you are working who usually looks after the baby?

PLEASE TICK __ONE__ BOX ONLY

No-one apart from me ☐ 1

Husband or partner ☐ 2

Mother or mother-in-law ☐ 3 ⎤

Childminder ☐ 4 ⎥→ (a)

Nursery or creche ☐ 5 ⎥

Someone else (please tick and write in) ☐ 6 ⎦

12

(a) Do you pay to have the baby looked after?

Yes ☐ 1

No ☐ 2

13

36. When you look back on how you have fed your baby since his/her birth are you happy with everything you decided to do or do you wish that you had made other decisions about how to feed him/her?

I am happy with my decisions ☐ 1 → Q37

I wish I had made other decisions ☐ 2 → (a)

14

(a) Looking back, what decisions would you have made?

MC=3

15
16
17

15

Please do not write in this column

18

37. Is there anything else you would like to say about feeding your baby?

Yes ☐ 1 ──→ please write in below

No ☐ 2

Please give the date when you filled in this questionnaire

day ☐   month ☐   year ☐ 19

WAS THERE ANYTHING YOU INTENDED TO GO BACK AND COMPLETE?   PLEASE CHECK.

Thank you very much for your help.

16

125

Covering letters

Office of Population Censuses and Surveys
St Catherines House 10 Kingsway London WC2B 6JP

Social Survey Division   Telephone 071-242 0262 ext   2325/2186
GTN 3042

Our reference S1299/E1/1

Your reference

Date   October 1990

Dear Madam

SURVEY OF INFANT FEEDING

I am writing to ask for your help in an enquiry into Infant
Feeding that is being carried out for the Department of Health,
since I understand that you have recently had a baby. A survey
on the same subject was carried out in 1985 and we want to find
out how practices have changed since then.

We would like to hear from mothers of young babies about how they
feed their babies. Since we cannot contact all mothers we have
selected names at random from the register of births and your
name has been included by chance in this selection.

I realise how busy you are at the moment with a new baby but I
would be very grateful if you could spare time to fill in the
enclosed questionnaire and return it in the envelope provided.

If, for any reason, your baby is no longer with you please tick
the box on the front page of the questionnaire and return it to
us so that we do not trouble you further.

As in all our surveys we rely on people's voluntary
co-operation. The information that you give is treated in strict
confidence by OPCS. It is not released to any other Government
department in any way in which it can be associated with your
name and address. No information about your household is ever
passed to any members of the public or press. In published
reports the identity of an individual is never released: the
results of the survey are shown as statistics only.

Thank you in advance for your help.

Yours faithfully

Amanda White
Senior Social Survey Officer

Office of Population Censuses and Surveys
St Catherines House 10 Kingsway London WC2B 6JP

Social Survey Division   Telephone 071-242 0262 ext   2325/2186

Our reference S1299/E2B/1

Your reference

Date   January 1991

Dear Madam

SURVEY OF INFANT FEEDING

We contacted you several months ago asking for your help with a
study of Infant Feeding which is being carried out for the
Department of Health. On that occasion you kindly completed our
questionnaire and I am writing to ask if you would help us again.

We are interested in finding out how the pattern of feeding
changes as babies get older and I am enclosing a questionnaire
about this which can be returned in the reply paid envelope
provided.

If, for any reason, your baby is no longer with you please tick
the box on the front page of the questionnaire and return it to
us so that we do not trouble you further.

As in all our surveys we rely on people's voluntary
co-operation. The information that you give is treated in strict
confidence by OPCS. It is not released to any other Government
department in any way in which it can be associated with your
name and address. No information about your household is ever
passed to any members of the public or press. In published
reports the identity of an individual is never released: the
results of the survey are shown as statistics only.

Thank you in advance for your help.

Yours faithfully

Amanda White
Senior Social Survey Officer

Office of Population Censuses and Surveys
St Catherines House 10 Kingsway London WC2B 6JP   Telephone 071-242 0262 ext 2325/2186

Social Survey Division

Our reference S1299/E3B/1

Your reference

Date June 1991

Dear Madam

SURVEY OF INFANT FEEDING

We contacted you twice over the last 9 months asking for your
help with a study on infant feeding which is being carried out
for the Department of Health. On both occasions you kindly
completed our questionnaire and I am now writing to ask if you
will help us with the final stage of the survey.

We are interested in how the pattern of feeding changes as babies
reach 9 to 10 months and I am enclosing a questionnaire about
this which can be returned in the reply paid envelope provided.

If, for any reason, your baby is no longer with you please tick
the box on the front page of the questionnaire and return it to
us so that we do not trouble you further.

As in all our surveys we rely on people's voluntary
co-operation. The information that you give is treated in strict
confidence by OPCS. It is not released to any other Government
department in any way in which it can be associated with your
name and address. No information about your household is ever
passed to any members of the public or press. In published
reports the identity of an individual is never released: the
results of the survey are shown as statistics only.

Thank you in advance for your help.

Yours faithfully

Amanda White

Amanda White
Senior Social Survey Officer

Printed in the United Kingdom for HMSO
Dd296325 4/93 C10 G3397 10170

127